David Brandon
with Althea and Toby Brandon

VENTURE PRESS 1995

Published by
VENTURE PRESS
16 Kent Street
Birmingham
B5 6RD
Tel: 0121 622 3911

First published 1995

British Library Cataloguing-in-Publication Data.
A catalogue record for this book is available from the British
Library.

ISBN 187 3878 141 (paperback)

Printed and bound in Great Britain by
Biddles Ltd, Guildford and King's Lynn

CONTENTS

Preface

PREFACE

As a family, we have been involved with advocacy for more than thirty years, both on the doing and on the receiving ends. We have known mental illness, physical disability and serious physical illness. We have known fear and vulnerability and the infinite complexities of involvement with services and professionals. This book is written mainly out of those experiences for people who have a variety of disabilities and the professionals who work alongside them.

It was begun 3 years ago with a small study on peer support and peer advocacy in the mental health field financed by the Mental Health Foundation. We are grateful to them and, in particular, to Cynthia Fletcher. We also owe a considerable debt to Karen Campbell from the Manic Depressive Fellowship; Paul Walsh; Jane Akister from Anglia Polytechnic University; Edna Conlan of the National Advocacy Network; Vanda Margarit from Bucharest, Romania; Steve Dowson and Andrew Holman, both formerly of Values into Action and now available for hire; Peter Campbell from Survivors Speak Out, and a very wide variety of advocacy projects; Andrew Dunning; Philippa Russell of the Council for Disabled Children, whose wonderfully helpful notes on the family advocacy chapter were almost longer than the chapter itself; Peter Durrant of Cambridgeshire Social Services and Dr Shula Ramon of the London School of Economics. Our debt to Professor Wolf Wolfensberger, the great visionary of advocacy, with whom we have so many disagreements, is evident on every page. It is our fault alone that this work is not much better.

In writing this book we began by exploring a country where we are frequent travellers. At the beginning, we felt that some parts would be very familiar and others would seem more foreign, even hostile. Through our journeying, we have discovered new continents or even galaxies and most have seemed foreign and strange to us. Even the central terms of disability and advocacy tend to retreat into the mist, the more they receive analysis. We are left with a whole range of questions and very few answers. a further ten thousand places to explore. One lifetime is hardly enough.

This small book is dedicated passionately to all those who advocate - whether users or providers or both and the human costs they pay. We know just a little of those costs. We have some wounds and scars ourselves. In particular, health and social services usually defend themselves mightily against outsiders and also insiders - the

i

whistleblowers - who speak out for those devalued and marginalised. The services defend mostly through personal abuse. We salute all the people who bring about genuine changes in transferring power to people with disabilities. May this book send much deserved strength and hope to advocates everywhere.

David Brandon
Althea Brandon
Toby Brandon
Anglia Polytechnic University,
Cambridge

Winter 1994

ONE: INTRODUCTION

"What experience and history teach is this - that people and governments never have learned anything from history, or acted on principles deduced from it." (1)

ORIGINS

In this text, we are concerned about advocacy for people with disabilities. **Advocacy involves a person(s), either an individual or group with disabilities or their representative, pressing their case with influential others, about situations which either affect them directly or, and more usually, trying to prevent proposed changes which will leave them worse off.** Both the intent and the outcome of such advocacy should increase the individual's sense of power; help them to feel more confident, to become more assertive and gain increased choices.

There are only three basic kinds of advocacy, although adopting many different forms - **self** by the person directly affected; **paid/professional** and **unpaid/amateur**. Professional advocacy has an extremely long lineage - largely through solicitors and barristers and more latterly through the Scandinavian tradition of Ombudsman. Some legal advocates also work to define and implement the rights of disabled people.

The majority of us will need paid advocates from time to time, whether in the form of a solicitor for an alleged motoring offence or of an accountant to keep the Inland Revenue from taking away our belongings or from a trade union representative to help at an industrial tribunal. We will need trained and competent people, familiar with the various relevant and complex systems, who can articulate the case for our 'fair' treatment. Preferably they will be independent, 'take our instructions' and continually inform about what is happening. Perhaps the starkest definition of this form of advocacy was provided by the seventeenth-century Speaker of the House of Commons. When asked to meet with his monarch - Charles I - he refused the invitation, replying bravely: *"I have neither eye to see, nor tongue to speak here, but as the House is pleased to direct me."* (2) He saw himself as simply a messenger.

Unpaid and amateur advocacy developed early, certainly before the parable of the Good Samaritan. (3) The Book of Common Prayer asks boldly of God to be 'Our Mediator and Advocate'. (4) Spielberg's marvellous film 'Schindler's List' celebrates the effective and unpaid advocacy of the business man Oscar Schindler, apparently working with an immensely oppressive system, rescuing some Jews from the Nazis. Disabled people have been speaking out on their own behalf for hundreds of thousands of years, long before it was termed 'self-advocacy'. Families defended their disabled members before the development of speech. A more recent growth is the army of volunteer advocates in various guises like 'citizen advocacy'.

Advocacy is partly a device to influence the balance of the needs/rights of the group in the favour of the needs/rights of individuals, especially those on the social margins. In the last century, John Stuart Mill wrote: 'The principle is, that the sole end for which mankind are warranted, individually or collectively, in interfering with the liberty of action of any of their number is self-protection. That the only purpose for which power can be rightfully exercised over any member of a civilised community, against his will, is to prevent harm to others. His own good, either physical or moral, is not a sufficient warrant. He cannot rightfully be compelled to forbear because it will be better for him to do so, because it will make him happier, because, in the opinion of others, to do so would be wise or even right. There are good reasons for remonstrating with him, but not for compelling him, or visiting him with an evil in case he does otherwise. To justify that, the conduct from which it is desired to deter him must be calculated to produce evil in someone else.' (5)

Mill went on to make a major qualification: ". . . this doctrine is meant only to human beings in the maturity of their faculties and specifically excludes those who are still in a state to require being taken care of by others must be protected against their own actions as well as against external injury." (6) That would seem to exclude a great many people who constitute the subject of our book.

Dworkin defines the rights of some people with dementias, presumably excluded by Mill: '. . . consider the rights, not of someone who was born and always has been demented, but of someone who has been competent in the past. We may think of that person, as the putative holder of rights, in two different ways: as a demented person, in which case we emphasise his present situation and capacities, or as a person who has become demented, in which case we emphasize that his dementia has occurred in the course of a larger life whose length must be considered in any decision about what rights he has.' (7)

That principle is only just a beginning. We need to build on the lives of those who have had no 'before' only an 'after'. In advocating for Judith, who has been multiply disabled from birth and without speech, I tried hard to sense the sort of person she is and might become. She had already been manipulated by many powerful others. I tried to put my own feelings and inclinations aside, which was hard to do. By following her around over days and weeks, I got some glimmer of what she was and might become and, out of that, attempted to write down some visions for her. (8)

OPPRESSION

People with disabilities need a clearer definition of rights because they struggle against hugely oppressive forces. Wolfensberger shows in his seminal work on the principle of normalisation, that they are devalued in most societies. (9) Historically they have been perceived as sub-human, defective, objects of charity and infectious. Take this example: 'The term "disabled women" can quickly and easily be substituted with the words "defective women". In a society which places substantial emphasis on "feminine" attractiveness and the ability to take care of one's own basic bodily functions, disabled women are dealt a severe blow. One disabled woman writes, "I had this image of myself as a big blob, no shape just dead meat". (10)

The most horrific depths of this process were the dehumanisation and mass murder of disabled people during the Nazi period. Hoche argued that mental patients were simply 'human ballast' and 'useless eaters'. (11) The 'philosophy' of 'Tödliches Mitleid' (deadly compassion) justified the killing of hundreds of thousands of hospital patients. Such savage processes simply lie dormant. During the 1950s, hundreds of mentally retarded patients in the Massachusetts Fernald institution were fed radioactive milk in a nutrition study sponsored by the Atomic Energy Commission and Quaker Oats. They were not informed or consulted about the radiation. Many have since developed cancer and died prematurely. (12)

In Britain, we have few grounds for complacency. In 1931, an influential British psychiatrist wrote: 'The out and out lunatic can be controlled and his injurious influence circumscribed, but the half-mad is practically unrestrained and free to go about broadcasting trouble and perplexity. There is, I believe, scarcely a family in these days that does not include some psychopathic or neuropathic member, not certifiable, passing muster as a self-regulating human being, often as one who is injured and misunderstood, but who is more or less or from time to time abnormal, difficult, irritable, depressed,

3

suspicious, capricious, eccentric, impulsive, unreasonable, cranky, deluded, and subject to all kinds of imaginary maladies and nervous agitations, thus diffusing discomfort and perturbation around . . . It must be a long wait, but Eugenism must do something toward the elimination of these half-mads.' (13)

On less terrible levels, the perception of disabled people as not fully human or even subhuman involved the wholesale abuse of their rights, best epitomised by the psychiatric and mental handicap hospital scandals in the 1970s. Without continued intervention to accentuate positive values, the services can easily ferment a poisonous brew of sexism, racism and ablism with a huge handful of paternalism thrown in for good measure. Such services become excessively concerned with enforcing compliance rather than about enhancing liberties. (14)

Donnison outlines this eloquently: '. . . the people most likely to be deprived of rights are the powerless; the people whose interests can most safely be neglected by the powerful. And the rights they are most likely to want will be things which the powerful already have, and do not wish to surrender: jobs, at a rate of pay which was pushed up partly by keeping other people out of them; decent housing, in neighbourhoods made more attractive by keeping other people out; an education for their children which gives them an inside track in the race to success.' (15)

Ablism, as this form of discrimination is termed, exists in the context of discrimination against other relatively powerless groups like women and ethnic minorities. Some are doubly and trebly discriminated against. For example, in the field of mental health: 'Studies over the past twenty years show that black people are more likely than white to be - removed by the police to a place of safety under section 136 of the Mental Health Act 1983; retained in hospital under sections 2, 3 and 4 of the Act; diagnosed as suffering from schizophrenia or another form of psychotic illness; detained in locked wards of psychiatric hospitals; given higher dosages of medication.' They are less likely than white people to receive 'appropriate and acceptable diagnosis or treatment for possible "mental illness" at an early stage; receive treatments such as psychotherapy and counselling.' (16)

The roots of such discrimination arise partly out of the neglect and ignorance of the relevant professionals and their structures. For example, social services departments can be an inexcusable mystery to minority groups. In 1994, a survey of ethnic minority families in south-east Hampshire showed that black communities still had serious difficulties in gaining access to social services and that

4

their needs went largely unmet. The majority of families had not heard of the local social services department; and more than a third of those who had, did not know what services were offered. (17)

Ablism, like racism and sexism, reflects fundamental issues of prejudice and economic inequality. 'Black people's experience of racism cannot be compartmentalised and studied separately from the underlying social structure; women's experience of sexism cannot be separated from the society in which it takes place; and neither can disabled people's experience of disablism and inequality be divorced from the society in which we all live. That society is characterised by fundamental inequalities and by ideologies which divide people against each other - the experience of disability is an integral part of this.' (18)

RIGHTS

There has been an insidious tendency for service users to internalise this oppression. They learn to see themselves simply as 'problems' to be somehow solved by the 'experts'. Professionals are increasingly cast, often willingly, in the role of rescuers saving people from their own foolish selves. (19)

Advocacy has an important role in the overall movement to identify the major causes of unnecessary suffering as external to the individual. It promotes an increased awareness of rights and participation - rejects paternalism and moves towards greater political involvement. This leads directly to a struggle with the various professionals, often seen as oppressors; increasing demands for anti-discrimination legislation; and for greater involvement in both the planning and running of services - the discovery of the disabled person as an active citizen.

Community care professionals, historically seen as the 'goodies' are increasingly vilified. For example: 'They [i.e. health professionals] are the gate-keepers who control the use of resources available to people designated as "patients" or "clients" through the National Health Service and the social services. Black and ethnic minorities are deprived of their rightful share of these resources because the structure and content of these resources are often irrelevant to their needs or exclude them selectively through racism and cultural insensitivity at various levels.' (20)

Or to take a more benevolent view: 'Doctors are not making more mistakes but a more open climate is encouraging patients and the medical profession to speak out when something goes wrong'.

'Certainly the climate has changed dramatically in the past ten years. What is happening is that both patients and doctors are more inclined to recognise that when something goes wrong it is not just a matter for the individual but something of public interest,' according

5

to Christine Tomkins of the Medical Defence Union. 'We are also seeing that doctors and patients are more ready to recognise that their treatment is a question of agreement. All this points to the fact that patients are more ready to question what happens to them.' (21)

In the move towards increased participation, an important force is the Independent Living movement (I.L.). It arose during the late 1970s in the United States, as more and more 'patients' moved out of institutions, 'demanding greater independence and broader social participation for disabled persons. Along with accessible housing, supporting services, and assistive devices, a greater degree of self-determination was sought as a move away from dependency'. (22) 'The IL concept provides a new perception of people with disabilities. In contrast to the more passive images given disability by the medical and rehabilitation models, the IL concept presents the disabled person as capable of political advocacy, self-help, and consumer control of services.' (23) This projected a much more active vision of disabled individuals.

The Americans with Disabilities Act (ADA) became law in July 1990 and was the major success for the Disability Movement and its powerful collective advocacy. ADA makes it illegal to discriminate against anyone who has a disability - in employment, public services, transportation, telecommunications and access . It provided a machinery for enforcement. The most notable improvements have been in accommodation because the lack of physical access to buildings is easier to understand. It has had a considerable knock-on effect by increasing the visibility of disabled people.

ADA has helped increased integration especially in the access and employment areas. A 'USA Today' editorial in July 1993: 'Braille dots are popping up next to numbers on automatic teller machines. Phones for the deaf are being established in sports arenas. Employers are scratching questions about medical problems from application forms. From offices to movie theatres, the impact of the most sweeping piece of civil rights legislation ever enacted is being seen, heard and felt . . .' (24)

The British independent living movement developed similar ideas and also pressed for fresh legislation. The formation of the British Council of Organisations of Disabled People (BCODP) in 1981 provided a national forum for bringing together relevant ideas. (25) Consciousness-raising became a key objective. 'Disabled people as a collective force have, through the disability rights movement, used the experiences and understanding of disability as social oppression to: (a) challenge the professional and public perceptions of disability as being a natural consequence of a biological condition; and (b) demand

6

the right to self-determination and full and equal participation in the social, economic and political sphere.' (26) This was the start of a huge shift from passive gratitude to assertive action which met with resistance from many service professionals.

The cry from groups of people with disabilities was increasingly for 'rights not care'. The battle was against discrimination - everything from lack of access for people in wheelchairs to cinemas; to transport problems and employment issues. This struggle took place against a background of international declarations defining rights. For example, the United Nations Declaration on the Rights of Mentally Retarded Persons defined the rights to personal advocacy, to protection from abuse and degrading treatment and to proper legal safeguards against any unwarranted restriction of rights. (27) These declarations were all the more remarkable because their demands were so banal.

Seeming legislative success, sometimes turned into pyrrhic victory. The British Disabled Persons (Services, Consultation and Representation) Act got to the statute book in 1986. It gave people with a disability the rights to representation, to assessment, to information and to consultation. (28) Over the next few years, most of this was placed in cold storage by a Conservative government which saw it as unnecessary and expensive. 'The recent decision not to implement sections 1, 2 and 3 of the 1986 Act demonstrates how little Government rhetoric has to do with reality.' (29) Conservatives stressed: 'individual rather than collective rights; rights conferring negative freedoms from restraints upon liberty, rather than positive freedoms to fulfil human potentiality; and rights calling for legal restraints upon the power of the state, rather than positive action which might change the odds under which different social groups compete.' (30)

There were some successes. The Children Act of 1989, introduced a new category of children in need, specifically including disabled children. "For the first time, disabled children were specifically included in children's legislation, integrated with other groups of children, rather than being included, almost by default, in legislation designed with adults in mind." "A child is disabled if he is blind, deaf or dumb or suffers from mental disorder of any kind or is substantially and permanently handicapped by illness, injury or congenital deformity or such disability as may be prescribed."(31)

In general, these fine words usually meant little to the everyday lives of disabled individuals. Across the world, people with disabilities had few rights and little redress. For example: "Psychiatric patients lose the right to vote in Japan, India and, in some instances, in Britain and the USA. In Holland, Egypt and many European countries, they lose the right to administer their own property. In Japan, Egypt and Israel they lose the right to write and receive uncensored mail. In most countries, outside America, patients do not have the right to refuse treatment." (32)

Campaigners saw themselves drowning in an ocean of oppression swept by huge waves of pity, compassion and welfare. 'Not only has state welfare failed to ensure the basic human rights of disabled people, but it has also infringed and diminished some of these rights. It has done this, for example, by providing segregated residential facilities which deny some disabled people the right to live where they choose, and by imposing assessment procedures which deny some disabled people the right to privacy.' (33) They were heavily influenced by currents in the linked struggles against racism and sexism. 'Disability is a human rights issue requiring political action rather than a social problem requiring welfare provision.' (34)

Rogers and Pilgrim usefully compare the ten points of principle set out by the National Council for Civil Liberties (renamed Liberty) with the existing situation of psychiatric patients. Take the first principle: 'The right to live in freedom and safe from personal harm . . .' 'The Mental Health Act 1983 has done nothing to reduce compulsory admissions. In fact, the number of people compulsorily detained has increased since the implementation of the Act. . . . The eighth principle is the right to freedom of peaceful assembly and association . . .' 'Both heterosexual and homosexual contact is restricted or banned in psychiatric hospitals. The more coercive the regime, the more likely that such segregation is strictly enforced. Patients may have to sleep in dormitories which do not provide the privacy required for intimate association.' (35)

In continental Europe, struggles for legal remedies against discrimination were heavily influenced by events in the United States. Unique in Europe, the French penal code contains provisions which render it a criminal offence to discriminate against a person on grounds of race, sex, nationality and religion on the provision of goods, services and employment etc. In July 1990, an Act included discrimination on the grounds of health or handicap. (36)

The campaign for legislation in Britain really caught alight in June 1994 with 2,000 people lobbying Parliament during an unsuccessful attempt to get the Civil Rights (Disabled Persons) Bill through. It was eventually 'talked out' by Government backbenchers. It tried to define disability and discrimination; to describe what activities would be covered by law; and how they would be enforced. The Government, whilst welcoming the basic principles, argued that it was prohibitively expensive - according to last minute estimates £17

billion.   Nicholas Scott, then Minister for the Disabled, said:
"Comprehensive anti-discrimination legislation would present practical difficulties, lead to increased litigation and unquantifiable costs
for business and taxpayers." (37)

PROCESS AND TASKS

Southgate sees five major tasks in the advocacy process - **nurturing, witnessing, protesting, translating** and **supporting**. (38)
People with disabilities are marginalised both socially and economi-
cally and learn to internalise that negativity. The advocate has an
important **nurturing** role. Advocates must learn to give emotional
and practical help in ways which are needed. Their clients may have
been through intense periods of deprivation and loneliness and need
appreciation, to be listened to carefully and be taken seriously.
Sometimes disabled people will have few relatives or friends and little money. They may have little reason to trust others. Meetings can
involve doing things together like going to the cinema or pub, learning about the other person, working towards feeling worthwhile;
asserting one's wishes.

The advocate must bear effective **witness** to the suffering and
maltreatment of the person he or she supports. One task of the witness is to note and record what happens to the partner, who has probably not been believed by powerful others. Lord Shaftesbury noted
the central dilemma in the early nineteenth century. 'What an awful
condition that of a lunatic ! His words are generally disbelieved, and
his most innocent peculiarities perverted; it is natural that it should
be so; we know him to be insane; at least we are told that he is so;
and we place ourselves on guard - that is, we give to every word,
look, gesture a value and meaning which oftentimes it cannot bear,
and which it would never bear in ordinary life.' (39)

From witnessing, the advocate **protests** about what is being done
to the person; about the devaluing and rejection. He or she amplifies
both the nature and degree of the suffering with a loud and clear
voice so that people can hear who have the power to change things.
The advocate shouts stop. The client must be seen as a valued individual. He or she is no longer alone but has an impassioned and
articulate defender, who doesn't just advocate but encourages them
to speak out on their own behalf, wherever possible.

Advocates **translate** and interpret the words and feelings of the
person to others as well as backing their partner directly. They must
know how to make that suffering understandable to those with
power. They have learned the professional terms and understand
some of the complexity of oppressive systems. Another important

interpreting function is to help the partner understand what happens to them in ordinary language.

Above all, advocates must **support** the inner advocacy and creativity of the individual. This is no ego trip. They can nourish the belief inside him/her that things can change for the better; the situation can be improved; there are some ways out of powerlessness. They support the power of the individual to speak out.

The opportunities for exploiting this precious process are infinite. For example, there is a considerable danger that advocacy becomes just another tool of professionals, another aspect of the multi-faceted service system. Various social workers, nurses and others may use it as another weapon in their struggle to hold onto or increase their own power. 'Professionals conceptualise advocacy in such a way as to maintain dominance and increase the use of that profession's services.' (40)

Another threat is the disappearance into a conceptual vacuum. Brown comments: 'Patients' rights advocacy as a concept needs to be rescued from its overgeneralisation.' (41) Wolfensberger warns fiercely against 'Kraft cheese advocacy', which devalues the term, simply adding it to traditional services. He defines its essential ingredients: 'Advocacy must involve some definite processes. It involves vigor and vehemence; it must cost something to the advocate; it must be free of conflict of interest.' (42)

The whole application of the advocacy concept to disability raises large questions. It is based on notions of rights and consumerism which are not easily made relevant. In this country, we are resistant to the spelling out of rights, although there have been some achievements in sexism and racism. More than a dozen attempts to establish rights for disabled people in Britain have been made, with little impact. (43) Widespread and deep patterns of ablism are dusted with the light sugar of caring paternalism.

Disabled people are not ordinary consumers. The services they use in health and social services are mainly monopolies; they have little access to cash to make the effective choice of 'voting with your feet'. Generations of professionals in residential care are accustomed to seeing them as a cash crop. They have grown used to receiving both poor quality and inflexible supports. The whole notion of 'patient' and 'client' conjures images of essentially passive and grateful individuals.

The advocacy process is essentially reactive. We tend to close the stable door after the horse has bolted. We are usually engaged in seeking redress after the wrongs have been done. We need to continue to defend partners but also to develop structures which are hopefully

10

more preventive and proactive.

Even the term 'disability' raises difficult issues. It is traditionally linked with pain and stigma. Those who were previously described as mentally handicapped now struggle to be identified as people with a 'learning difficulty' not a 'learning disability'. Many in the Deaf community resist the whole usage of disability. Nevertheless it is difficult to construct any alternative and general generic term which describes the situation. Concepts like 'differently abled' from politically correct speech seem merely pretentious nonsense with little meaning in the many different languages.

INTENTIONS

We have chosen to divide this book into the various types of advocacy rather than, as more usual, between the types of client groups. This means we can put the advocacy in the foreground rather than the groups of the elderly, physically disabled, mentally ill . . . constructed mostly by the professionals. That leads to several difficulties. Each sort of advocacy subsumes some, if not all, of the other kinds. Lawyers are not only involved in the advocacy of individual cases but usually have a collective advocacy purpose - to change the general nature of the rights for the whole group of people. We shall see an intimate interplay, even a substantial confusion, between the different terms - for example, between 'self-advocacy' and 'collective advocacy'.

We have looked closely at the developing **independent professional** tradition - the lawyer, the barrister, the ombudsman, increasingly the service-based advocates . . . What skills do they have ? How can the activities of these increasingly influential professionals be held firmly under the control of people with disabilities? They could easily be tempted into different kinds of imperialism.

The roles of **service professionals** like social workers and psychologists throw up some fascinating dilemmas for advocacy because they usually have so many other conflicting roles. We have looked especially at the whistleblowers, often reviled by the services they seek to change. What should these sorts of professionals do ? Can they have any kind of advocacy role without being seen as essentially destructive?

Families have been and are a primary support for people with disabilities, mostly from the female members - mothers and daughters. However, there are no free lunches and they are a source of suffering as well as liberation. The Hollywood film 'Lorenzos' Oil', the story of parents battling to find a cure for their mysteriously sick son, graphically illustrates those complexities.

The fundamental advocacy is that by people with disabilities themselves. To what extent are other forms of speaking out and on behalf of especially and paradoxically if effective - an actual hindrance? How do we balance tasks and processes in advocacy? How can we encourage individuals to recognise their oppression by others who may mean well and **speak up for themselves**? What about those who cannot speak for themselves - some of the dying; those with Alzheimer's Syndrome; those in a coma ...? Are there dangers that the other forms of advocacy can drown out the drive for 'speaking for ourselves' and develop other patterns of dependency?

Citizen advocacy originates in this technical form in the United States and has been struggling for a foothold in western Europe over the last fifteen years. It involves a volunteer working with a devalued person, and trying to provide friendship and representation, mainly in the learning difficulties field. Is it simply another form of clever, able-bodied colonialism? Is it just an expensive and pretentious befriending scheme?

Peer advocacy is rapidly expanding and attempts to support individuals who have been or currently are in similar situations as the advocate - for example, a psychiatric patient represents another patient; someone who was disabled in a serious road accident helps another to get through a rehabilitation programme; to rebuild their life. Can peer advocates be effective advocates without being reclientised and reclaimed by the system they once used?

Collective advocacy is an attempt to bring together people who have similar concerns to change legislation; to press government for more resources. It is concerned with political pressure through meetings and lobbying. Increasingly it centres on the disability movement which is very disunited. It struggles to get passed a civil rights Bill for people with a disability. Can that struggle and campaign succeed and how? Can very stigmatised groups, devalued even within the disability world, like those people with learning difficulties, become genuinely accepted?

As we shall see from this work, there has been an regrettable trend for advocacy to splinter into fragments. It is pulled in so many diverse directions; towards both specialist client groups and the different methods. So in most towns and cities, we have this delicate and fragile advocacy process battling against almost overwhelming odds and concentrated on smaller and smaller pieces like, for example, a citizen advocacy project for elderly people fighting other fragments for the scarce resources.

References

(1) George Wilhelm Hegel from the introduction to the 'Philosophy of History' quoted in Bernard Shaw's preface to 'Heartbreak House'

(2) Speaker William Lenthall in Rushworths Historical Collections, iv 238

(3) See for example in Wolf Wolfensberger's 'A Multi-component advocacy/protection schema' Canadian Association for the Mentally Retarded, 1977 (Pge 3)

(4) The Book of Common Prayer: 'Prayers and Thanksgivings, upon several occasions'

(5) John Stuart Mill from the introduction to 'Liberty' 1859

(6) Quoted in Kathleen Jones and A.J. Fowles 'Ideas on Institutions' Routledge & Kegan Paul, 1984 (Pge 136)

(7) Ronald Dworkin 'Autonomy and the Demented Self' The Millbank Quarterly, vol 64, supplement 2, 1986

(8) David Brandon 'The Yin and Yang of Care Planning' Anglia Polytechnic University 1993

(9) The term seems to have been used first in Maria Montessori's 'The Secret of Childhood' when she writes of 'la normalizzazione del bambino' (pge 291) - about converting a disabled child to the normal, quoted in Wolf Wolfensberger - chapter four 'The Definition of Normalization' in R. Flynn and K.E. Nitsch 'Normalisation, social integration and community services' 1980. See for a succinct account and clear definition John O'Brien and Alan Tyne 'The Principle of Normalisation' CMH 1981 and for the change to social role valorisation Wolf Wolfensberger and Susan Thomas 'Program Analysis of Service Systems - implementation of normalisation goals' Second Edition, National Institute of Mental Retardation, 1983

(10) Nasa Begum 'Disabled Women and the Feminist Agenda' Feminist Review, no 40, 1992 (Pge 76)

(11) R. Lifton 'The Nazi Doctors' MacMillan 1986

(12) Tim Cornwell 'Life under the Cloud of America's "Nazi" tests' The Observer: 2 January 1994

(13) Sir James Crichton-Browne 'The Doctor's Second Thoughts' 1931, quoted in Roy Porter (Editor) 'The Faber Book of Madness' Faber 1991 (Pges 84-5)

(14) David Brandon 'Increasing Value - the implications of the principle of normalisation for mental health services' University College Salford, 1991

(15) David Donnison 'A Radical Agenda - after the New Rights and the Old Left' Rivers Oram Press, 1991 (Pge 71)

(16) Daphne Wood 'MIND's policy on Black and Minority Ethnic People and Mental Health' MIND (1993)

(17) 'Equal Voices' Portsmouth University, Spring 1993

(18) Jenny Morris 'Feminism and Disability' Feminist Review no 43, 1993 (Pges 57-70)

(19) Ivan Illich 'Medical Nemesis' Caldar & Boyars 1975 saw professionalism as iatrogenic, causing diseases both in an individual and systemic way.

(20) Northern Curriculum Development Project, 'Racist Psychiatry' in 'Improving Mental Health Practice' CCETSW 1993 (Pge 21)

(21) Celia Hall 'Open climate that leads to Patients speaking out' The Independent, 30 September 1993

(22) Nancy A. Brooks 'Self-Empowerment among Adults with Severe Physical Disability: a case study' Journal of Sociology and Social Welfare: vol 18 March 1991 (Pge 108)

(23) Nasa Begum 'Disabled Women and the Feminist Agenda" Feminist Review, no 40, 1992 (Pge 72)

(24) Victoria Scott 'Lessons from America - a study of the Americans with Disabilities Act' RADAR 1994

(25) Liberty and BCODP 'Access Denied: Human Rights and Disabled People' Liberty 1994

(26) Jenny Morris 'Community Care or Independent Living?' Joseph Rowntree Foundation 1993 (Pge 9)

(27) United Nations Declaration on the Rights of Mentally Retarded Persons, 1971

(28) William Bingley and Rachel Hurst 'Getting in on the Act' Thames TV 1987

(29) Mary Holland 'Rights not Rhetoric' Contact, RADAR, no 69, autumn 1991 (Pge 10)

(30) David Donnison Ibid (Pge 63)

(31) Laura Middleton 'Children First: working with children and disability' Venture Press, 1992 (Pges 61-2)

(32) David Cohen 'Forgotten Millions: the treatment of the mentally ill - a global perspective' Paladin 1988 (Pge 30)

(33) Michael Oliver quoted in Peter Beresford and Suzy Croft 'Citizen Involvement - a practical guide for Change' MacMillan 1993 (Pge 5)

(34) Anne Rogers and David Pilgrim 'Mental Health and Citizenship' in CCETSW 'Improving Mental Health Practice' 1993

(35) Ian Bynoe et al "Equal Rights for Disabled People' Institute for Public Policy Research, 1991 (Pge 31)

(36) Loi no. 90-602 of 12 July 1990

(37) 'Civil Rights, society's wrongs: disabled people fight discrimination' Professional Social Work, May 1994 (Pges 8-9)

(38) John Southgate 'Towards a Dictionary of Advocacy based Self Analysis' Journal of the Institute for Self Analysis, vol. 4 no 1 December 1990

(39) Shaftesbury Diaries, 18 November 1844

(40) Neal Milner 'The Symbols and Meanings of Advocacy' International Journal of Psychiatry and Law, 1985

(41) Phil Brown 'The Transfer of Care - Psychiatric De-institutionalisation and its Aftermath' Routledge & Kegan Paul, 1985

(42) Wolf Wolfensberger 'A Multi-component advocacy/protection Schema' CAMR 1977 (Pge 18-21)

(43) Victoria Scott ibid (Pge 36)

TWO: PROFESSIONAL ADVOCATES

"A man can estrange himself from himself by mystifying himself and others. He can also have what he does stolen from him by the agency of others."(1)

There is a long and distinguished history of various kinds of professional advocates working to extend and implement the rights of people with disabilities both through representing individuals as well as in lobbying for general changes in the law. These include - ombudsmen of various kinds, specialist lawyers and barristers, MPs and other elected representatives, priests and, more recently, a rapidly increasing number and variety of non-legal but professional advocates, mainly attached to services.

LEGAL

Perhaps the foremost legal advocate for people with mental health problems is Larry Gostin, formerly of MIND and latterly of Harvard University, who became a psychiatric patient for three months in North Carolina's infamous institution for the criminally insane. He had false papers charging him with rape. 'I couldn't believe it when I saw it. The day room was the size of a largish sitting room and there were 15 to 20 men inside. There was a television high up on one side of the room and next to the television were three toilets with no doors! There were a few chairs scattered about and the whole place was filthy. Flies were buzzing everywhere.'

On discharge, he began a series of law suits against the North Carolina State - all successful. The first was brought on behalf of a long term patient he had met in the inside. The second suit concerned liberalising visiting - he had not been permitted to see his family or friends. The last suit involved a deal with State officials who agreed that he should draft a statute on compulsory admissions and in-patient rights. (2)

This initiative was part of a large scale involvement of legal groups in the USA, attempting to extend the rights of disabled people, reflecting the successes of the civil rights movement in the 1960s. (3) Over the past two decades, much advocacy on behalf of mentally retarded citizens focused on securing legal rights. 'The impetus for this trend was derived from a few major court rulings in favor of handicapped people. The trend toward the use of litigation to procure constitutional and statutory guarantees for persons with mental retardation is well established and will continue.' (4)

The New York civil liberties organisation began in the 1970s, a vast national project of litigation 'to protect and expand the rights of mental patients through court action at both state and federal level'. (5) For example in the State of New Jersey, a department of the Public Advocate was created in 1974, providing a wide range of legal services for those in psychiatric facilities and representing individual patients concerning their admission, detention and discharge. (6)

Rubenstein suggests that mental health legal advocacy is entering 'a second generation'. 'In the past, the legal and medical perspectives on issues relating to compulsory treatment focused on the individual's interest in liberty on the one hand and the physician's authority to treat on the other. Neither of these perspectives addresses the contemporary realities of treatment of chronically mentally ill people in the United States ... The record of advocacy for quality services, whether internal or external to institutions, however, far from being nihilistic, is one in which lawsuits have played an important role in enlarging the availability to patients of decent care, helping to supply funds for that care, ensuring accountability for that care.' (7)

One strand of that considerable pressure lies in the rapidly expanding field of medical negligence. 'The standard of care, and whether the defendant has failed to meet that standard, are normally the central issues in an action for medical negligence ...' (8) Court cases about negligence are preoccupied with issues of 'reasonable care'. The downside of such actions is the development of what is termed 'defensive medicine', doctors taking no risks, even where they might benefit the patient.

American influences became especially strong in Britain, through Tony Smythe, who became MIND Director in the early 1970s, and Gostin, recruited to head its legal services department. MIND fought important battles over the rights of individual detained patients, many in Broadmoor, a secure hospital for the criminally insane, all the way to the European Court of Human Rights. (9) It gradually redefined the central issues of mental health in terms of rights rather than care. Over roughly a decade ending in the early eighties, MIND had a seriously imbalanced strategy, focusing mainly on a relatively few patients in the special hospitals. A small number of test cases were successfully pursued, amid considerable publicity, but successful litigation had little influence on the conditions faced by the vast majority of people using the mental health services.

Rogers and Pilgrim are very critical: '. . . two cautions need to be made about the use of a narrow civil liberties perspective in mental health debates. First, there are no ready answers to the complex existential questions which arise for social actors in mental health crises. At times, maybe the disruptive behaviour of one person may constrain the civil rights of others. In such circumstances the demand for the curtailment of liberty may be quite understandable, though this may be actually warranted for only a tiny percentage of those currently incarcerated . . . Second, although a civil libertarian perspective helps to reveal the actual quality of life of the recipients of psychiatric services, and to set this against the rhetoric of professionals and politicians, there is a danger that civil rights for patients become the limited formula for mental health policy. For instance, Gostin's civil-libertarian leadership within MIND in the early 1980s helped to shape an individualistic legalistic policy solution to the exclusion of questions about the collective social needs of patients.' They conclude that the Mental Health Act of 1983, inspired by MIND, had done 'little to improve the status of mental health patients'.(10)

This particular caselaw tradition continues in other fields and needs to be one part of a many-pronged strategy. For example: 'A disabled man has used the courts to force his local authority to provide him with a carer, setting an important precedent for the forthcoming community shake-up. Hereford and Worcester County Council has agreed to provide the carer and pay the man £7,000 costs and £750 compensation after he won leave for a judicial review of his case in what is believed to be the first legal move of its kind.'(11)

Another example: Mark Hazell, 22 years old, has Downs Syndrome and lives an independent family life. He chose a relatively expensive Oxfordshire home for a long-term placement. The Avon County Council, where his family lives, refused to pay the fees and found alternative, and, in the view of his family, unsuitable accommodation. His advocate Richard Mills said: 'The initial assessment was woefully inadequate. It regarded Mark's needs as being very slight. Many of the proposals were subsequently based on that assessment.' Mark went to law to challenge the Avon assessment and in the High Court, Judge Henry found in his favour. (12)

The Law Society initiated a general debate on the law relating to vulnerable groups. In 1989 they published a document on mental incapacity and decision making and described the existing legislation as 'complicated, inflexible and piecemeal' concluding that reform was urgently needed. '. . .provision should be made for the development of advocacy schemes, allowing for both self-advocacy and citizen advocacy and requiring local authorities, health authorities, the courts and others to recognise as an advocate a representative appointed by or acting on behalf of the dependent person.' (13) In response, the Law Commission published a consultation paper acknowledging that the role of independent advocates was 'still in an embryonic stage' but 'support for the idea is, nevertheless, still growing'. (14)

The Group for Solicitors with Disabilities, founded in 1990, is concerned that 'proper rights be given to disabled individuals'. It finds inspiration in the American Disabilities Act and wants to see how it works and lessons applied to this country. 'We think many employers and organisations would welcome a statutory measure which defined more closely what was meant by disability in employment terms'. (15)

In general, legal intervention is reactive. Primarily it tries to stop things from happening. Its force 'lies in its power of injunction: it can override the timetable of political decisions, while new information is brought to bear on the argument, or issues reconsidered in a new light. And the court examines the issues on the plaintiff's terms, irrespective of the political authority of the parties: at least in principle, government and citizens are equal before the law. But this power of injunction, which enables anyone with a plausible case to threaten the political leadership with obstruction, is mainly negative'. (16)

Herr reminds us that legal intervention brings problems: 'Lawyers have the potential to dominate their developmentally disabled clients and usurp decisions that non-disabled clients would expect to make. This risk stems from several factors. The number of such practitioners is still limited. The clients are frequently impoverished, often depending on free, low-cost or contingent fee services to gain access to the justice system. Furthermore the temptation to be paternalistic is enormous . . .' (17) Lawyers have big egos as well and are often inexperienced in communicating with people who have disabilities. The movement from domination by care professionals to domination by lawyers can consist in simply swapping one form of tyranny for another. The numbers of private legal practices specialising in disability cases in Britain is increasing rapidly and so this may become an increasing problem.

OMBUDSMAN

The tradition of the Ombudsman, deeply rooted in the legal field, originates in Scandinavia. (18) This employs investigators in an agency guaranteeing maximum independence, attached to a legislative branch of government and provided with considerable powers to gather the facts. It is initiated through the complaint of a citizen. For example, 'The Norwegian Children's Ombudsman has the right and obligation to criticize any administrative level, any group, organization or person disregarding the interests of children, regardless of political or other considerations. This means that we can raise issues that may be difficult or impossible for others, such as employees of the municipal or governmental establishment, who are often bound to loyalty to the political leadership'. (19)

In the United States, the Long-Term Care (LTC) ombudsman was set up when the Older Americans Act was amended in 1978 out of public concern at poor conditions in the private nursing homes. Each state has a programme. LTC services vary considerably but many use volunteer advocates to support the work of full-time staff, particularly at a local level. (20)

We now have ombudsmen for both local authority and health services in this country which look into issues of maladministration. For example, 'there was an unreasonable delay in providing a disabled man with specific aids that would have improved the quality of his life. The council then failed to deal properly with the man's complaint about this and failed to apply the statutory services complaints procedure. The complainant felt the council had victimised him as a disabled person and had ignored his complaints. His ability to cope with the distressing symptoms of his illness was impaired'. The Local Government Ombudsman recommended that the complainant should be paid £500 compensation and that procedures be reviewed. (21)

The Health Services Ombudsman strongly criticised the new NHS arrangements. 'Far too often I have to deplore the treatment of patients which shows disregard for the needs and care of fellow humans. Far too often nothing has been done to manage patient care properly until I have completed an investigation . . . Many complaints have been caused by failure in communication. Some of these failures have been aggravated by splitting health care into many more separate organisations whose staff need more training for their responsibilities. Often staff are ignorant of the advice given by health departments about how to admit patients, how to give them adequate care and how to discharge them at the end of their period in hospital. Ignorance or an omission to put into practice well thought out guidance can lead to failures to provide the standards of care to which patients are entitled.' (22)

SERVICE ADVOCATES

In a number of European countries there is a long and well-established tradition of paid advocates. The Swedish law on guardianship and trusteeship provides people with mental health needs and learning difficulties with the assistance of a paid and independent spokesperson, inspired by their Ombudsman tradition. (23)

In the Netherlands, there are thirty three patient's advocates attached to psychiatric hospitals, managed by the independent National Foundation for Patient's Advocates (PA). They cover all forty-two Dutch mental hospitals, housing about 20,000 patients. The Dutch term 'patientenverstrouwenspersoon' literally means patient's confidant. All hospitals are obliged to pay a fixed amount towards funding the advocates, who are employed by the Foundation. They have a common training period, a published manual, standardised duties and working methods. They visit hospital wards and initiate conversations with patients. They are advisers/voices for individual patients but don't usually take up the more structural issues. (24) In the first six months of 1991, over 300 patients contacted an advocate. They complained most frequently about treatment and detention issues. Fifty per cent were dealt with by discussion between the advocate and the patient alone. In the other half, the PA negotiated with a staff member. In general, patients felt positive about the service. Hospital staff found it difficult to deal with the 'true advocacy' of the service, particularly when it interfered with treatments. (25)

In this country, there are no real equivalents to the Dutch advocates. The majority of the ninety-two Mental Health Act Commissioners set up by the Mental Health Act of 1983 are part-time service professionals as well. They have special powers and responsibilities to oversee only the conditions of detained patients. (26) The Commission's good code of practice has no direct legal force. (27)

In 1977, Community Health Councils (CHCs) were established to represent health service users. (28) The local CHC is the independent NHS consumer council. It encourages local groups to get involved with the NHS; carries out surveys and makes recommendations about proposed changes. It is especially concerned in helping people to complain. It helps them formulate the complaint and ensures it is followed up. In some cases, their staff go to the hearings. (29) Bradford CHC received 142 in part of 1992-3 - from problems of car parking to the alleged maiming and death of a relative. It employs two specialist advocates - one for people with learning disabilities and another for elderly people. Both posts involve a lot of time spent training professionals and advising on management; not only involved with individuals but also with policy influencing processes. (30) This duality of roles is a mixed blessing. It may help make services more relevant to user needs but at the cost of co-opting advocates as team members.

Other developing strands have been citizen advice bureaux and the hospital based law centres. The Springfield Advice and Law Centre is attached to a mental hospital. 'During the ten years that the Law Centre has been open, we have assisted over 2,500 different people with around 5,000 problems. About half of these involved correspondence, negotiation and sometimes representation at courts or tribunals . . . We encourage and assist people to do as much as they can for themselves - letting them use the telephone to ring the Benefits Agency or providing paper, a desk and advice on drafting a letter. Sadly, however, it has to be acknowledged that in many instances a letter on headed paper or a telephone call from the Law Centre provokes a more favourable and polite response.' (31) This points out neatly the tensions between professional and self-advocacy.

The Springfield deaf unit posed difficult communication issues. Hearing advocates couldn't communicate effectively and were sometimes seen as oppressive. It proved difficult to get good interpreters. In the relatively small deaf community, some interpreters 'who might come into contact with our potential clients in their primary professional capacity, had to be excluded because of a possible conflict of interest'. (32)

The Children and Young Persons Act 1969 gave children in care, or their carers, the right to involve an independent person - a guardian ad litem (GAL) - in a formal complaints investigation. This meant that someone outside the authority must hear the complaint and become involved in discussions. The statutory function of the 'guardian ad litem' is to safeguard the interests of the child. '. . . where feelings are running high and where there may be concern about possible injustices to the natural parents, the guardian may be the only person who can speak objectively or authoritatively on behalf of the child.' He or she is an officer of the court, expected to advise on, for example, whether the child is of sufficient age and experience to consent to a medical examination or attend hearings; about the wishes of the child; different outcomes which may be achieved and which is likely to be best for the child. (34) The GAL does not represent the child but seeks to present a non-partisan view of the child's welfare. However, the GAL can appoint a solicitor to act for the child. (33)

In October 1991, Voice for the Child in Care set up an Independent Person Service in response to the Children Act, 1989. It provides 20 local authorities and nine voluntary societies with independent persons (IPs). Forty-one IPs were recruited and trained for the London based service. A significant minority of the forty-two complaints in which the IPs were involved were about the use of restraint. (35) Advocacy Services for Children and Young People (ASC) aims 'to empower all children and young persons' and more specifically to enable children and young people being cared for by local authorities and voluntary agencies to effectively use the complaints mechanisms . . . by providing support, advice and the use of advocacy techniques, where they have identified a failure in the service being offered to them. Advocate's roles are listed as: listening to the young person; discussing the consequences of any proposed action; clarifying the issues; establishing the legal position; attempting to solve the problem through mediation and discussion. (36)

In 1991, the Spinal Injuries Association, funded by the Rowntree Foundation, set up an independent living advocacy project at Stoke Mandeville Hospital. 'The principle of advocacy is that it is the client who is at the centre of operations.' This full-time advocate helped with: sorting out housing problems; meeting personal needs; writing a personal needs plan; recruiting personal assistants; concerns about personal relationships; resolving conflicts experienced by patients within the hospital. (37)

A Brighton project serviced people who were both elderly and mentally ill. 'Involvement, consultation and empowerment are relatively recent concepts in mental health care for elderly people . . . The project linked the process of befriending with advocacy. Prior to representation it was felt that the confidence of the elderly person had to be won, which included gaining an understanding of the individual's needs and wishes. To some extent the process of befriending became an end in itself. Many of the elderly people who were referred did not want issues taken up or changes made in the service that they received; however, 'they did want me to visit and talk with them.' In the first six months, there were sixteen referrals; seven people were represented. People 'tended to be passive and grateful'.

The issues raised included: 'food, behaviour of some other patients, worries about the security of possessions; transport services; operation of the Mental Health Act; lack of privacy; loss of clothing in laundry services.' (38)

A growing number of so-called independent advocates are paid directly by service providers. Manmohan Bajwa, the manager of an interpreting service in Greenwich, jointly funded by the health authority and the social services department, comments: 'We have three full time interpreters, and seventy-eight sessional interpreters. We recruit interpreters through interview, and want them to act as advocates for people as well as interpreters. I need people who are well aware of the needs of the community with a class awareness too. They should have some knowledge of social services before they start . . . Staff were sometimes reluctant to share information about the case with the interpreter, not appreciating that the interpreters are professionals and part of the directorate, bound by the same rules of confidentiality as they are.' (39) This communicates ignorance about the clash of vested interests between advocacy and the employment by the agencies presumably most complained about.

There were also some hospital patient representatives. Appointments were made at the Brighton and Frenchay NHS Trusts in July 1992 with two main tasks: to respond directly to patients and relatives who felt their concerns were not being satisfactorily resolved; to work with other staff to improve services so that they become more patient focused. For example, arising out of 'discussion with local black and minority ethnic groups led the patient representative to investigate why complaints were being made about the food available. She found that although some of the appropriate food was stored in the freezers it did not appear on the menu because of "lack of demand." After discussions with the catering department, kosher and halal meals were put on the menu at every meal'. (40)

After a study showing that most patients felt excluded from decision-making, a ten-strong team of patient advocates was funded by Leeds City Council in 1987. The advocates work in the hospitals and clinics, accessible to any patient in Leeds and district. Former nurse Trina Glynn leads the team. 'Advocacy is necessary because there is an imbalance of power between the health service and its users. Members of the public find it hard to criticise or question.' This scheme is linked with interpreting services to reflect the diverse needs of the multi-cultural community. (41) It is hard to see how this local authority-funded service can safeguard it's crucial independence.

ISSUES

Legal advocates are increasingly concerned with the underlying causes of neglect and oppression - poor resourcing, high resident-to-staff ratios; untrained staff, poorly supervised and working long hours; institutional and inflexible systems of caring . . . Some are a powerful force inside collective advocacy, pressing in partnership with others like families and service users for better facilities, rather than obsessed by narrow legalism.

But lawyers also have their own colonialist and even dynastic ambitions. Few enter the disability field only with righteous compassion in their hearts. They want more money, status, power and control like other professionals. (42) Caplan argues that lawyers are simply employees of an élite and expensive cult. (43) Battles with doctors and other professionals through, for example, malpractice suits can serve simply to divert large sums into their ample pockets and those of a few aggrieved individuals. They need to aim for the transfer of power to disabled people, otherwise individuals as well as groups may find themselves simply going out of the frying pan into the fire.

The law has its own problems. A European study comments somewhat blandly: 'The interests of the severely disabled are not easily acknowledged in the political process that leads towards laws and administrative practice . . . They are a minority group with few advantages and few to speak for them, especially in times of economic difficulty . . . The health and socio-political actions that have been taken on behalf of disabled persons have been unduly narrow, promoting the impression that disabled persons are sick, unable to work and a special group requiring help and pity from the non-disabled section of society.' (44) More particularly, Perske suggests that the United States legal system has serious problems with the 'mentally retarded'. He argues that they are treated unequally before the law and suggests reasons for this discrimination. (45) Our Lord Chief Justice recently accused the criminal justice system of 'failing blacks and Asians by tolerating racist attitudes and allowing ethnic minorities to believe they were beyond the protection of the law.' (46)

Non-legal professional advocates attached to services have a difficult task in protecting precious independence. Current funding arrangements make that almost impossible, leaving them exposed to the service providers. Advocates can easily become infected by service cultures. They can get seduced into being almost a part of the service. Take this example from New Zealand: 'One of the first tasks that David, as Senior Development Advocate, will be concerned with is the establishment of friendship networks' and under the "request for services" procedure: It constitutes an agreement between the service provider and the advocate, who is then responsible for continuously monitoring the programme to ensure the continuity of service provision.' (47) This advocate has disappeared almost without trace into the service.

Arising out of the fragmented nature of advocacy in most countries, advocates can easily get trapped into simply seeking redress for individuals in contrast to attempting to remedy the structural defects. In a visit to the Netherlands, I was struck by the extent to which full-time advocates in mental hospitals were compelled to look at the individual manifestations of systemic oppression, rather than to examine the oppressive structures as a whole.

References:

(1) R.D. Laing 'The Politics of Experience and the Bird of Paradise' Penguin 1967 (Pge 25)

(2) David Brandon 'Voices of Experience - consumer perspectives of psychiatric treatment' MIND 1981 (Pge 8)

(3) Phil Brown (editor) 'Mental Health Care and Social Policy' Routledge 1985 (Pge 207)

(4) Craig Fiedler and Richard Antonak Chapter 2 in J.L. Matson and J.A. Mulick (Editors) 'Handbook of Mental Retardation' Pergamon Press, New York, 1986 (Pge 29)

(5) Peter Sedgwick 'Psycho Politics' Pluto 1982

(6) M.L. Perlin 'Mental patient advocacy by a patient advocate' Psychiatric Quarterly 1982; S4(3) (Pges 169-179)

(7) Leonard Rubenstein 'Treatment of the Mentally Ill: legal advocacy enters the second generation' American Journal of Psychiatry, 143:10 October 1986 (Pges 1264-1269)

(8) Michael A. Jones 'Medical Negligence' Sweet & Maxwell, 1991 (Pge 56)

(9) See for example Larry Gostin 'A Human Condition' MIND 1975

(10) Anne Rogers and David Pilgrim 'Mental Health and Citizenship' in 'Improving Mental Health Practice' CCETSW 1983 (Pge 97)

(11) David Brindle 'Care Test case ruling will help disabled' The Guardian 26 October 1991

(12) Catriona Marchant 'What Comes First?' 15 July 1993 (Pges 18-19)

(13) Law Society 'Decision-making and mental incapacity: a discussion document' Law Society's Mental Health sub-committee, 1989

(14) Law Commission 'Mentally incapacitated adults and decision-making: an overview' Law Commission consultation paper no 119, HMSO 1991 (paragraphs 6.48 - 6.49)

(15) John Willis 'Group for Solicitors with Disabilities' Contact, RADAR, no 69, autumn 1991 (Pge 44)

(16) Peter Marris and Martin Rein 'Dilemmas of Social Reform' Pelican 1974 (Pges 361-362)

(17) Stanley S. Herr 'Disabled Clients, constituencies and counsel: representing persons with Developmental Disabilities' The Millbank Quarterly, vol 67, Supplement 2, Part 2, 1989 (Pges 352-379)

(18) William B. Gwyn 'The Ombudsman in Britain: a qualified success in Government reform' Public Administration, vol 60, summer 1980 (Pges 177-195)

(19) Maalfrid Grude Flekkoy 'Child Advocacy in Norway: The Ombudsman' Child Welfare vol LXVIII, no ., March/April 1989 (Pges 113-128) and see also her 'A Voice for Children: speaking out as their Ombudsman' Jessica Kingsley Publishers 1991

(20) Quoted in Alison Wertheimer 'Speaking Out: citizen advocacy and older people' Centre for Policy on Ageing 1993 (Pges 7-8)

(21) 'The Local Government Ombudsman: annual report 1993-4' The Commission for Local Administration for England, 1994 (Pges 43-44)

(22) Annual report of the Health Service Commissioner 1993-4, HMSO 1994

(23) Access to Health 'The Tomato Sauce of the Health Service' November 1992

(24) David Brandon 'Innovation without Change?' MacMillan 1991 (pges 122-3)

(25) Marinus P. Klijnsma 'Patient advocacy in the Netherlands' Psychiatric Bulletin 17, 1993 (pp 230-231)

(26) Department of Health 'Mental Health Act - Code of Practice' HMSO. 1990

(27) David Carson 'Coded Messages on a Matter of Principle' The Health Service Journal, 18 January 1990

(28) Ruth Levitt 'The Peoples Voice in the NHS' Kings Fund 1980

(29) Association of Community Health Councils 'CHCs working for a better Health service' undated leaflet

(30) Bradford Community Health Council 'Annual Report 1992-3' 1993

(31) Springfield Advice and Law Centre 'Biennial Report' 1990-1992 and see also Kings Fund Project Paper 'The Advice and Representation Project at Springfield Hospital, 1982-1985', Number 59, 1986

(32) Springfield Advice and Law Centre 'Biennial Report' 1990-1992 (Pge 4)

(33) Margaret Adcock 'The role of the guardian ad litem' paper presented to the British Adopting and Fostering Association legal group seminar, April 1984

(34) Wendy Stainton Rogers and Jeremy Roche 'Children's Welfare & Children's Rights - a practical guide to the law' Hodder & Stoughton, 1994 (Pges 35-36)

(35) Kendra Sone 'Now Hear the Whimper of our Discontent' Community Care, 4 March 1993 (Pge 27)

(36) Advocacy Services for Children and Young People 'Information Sheet' Manchester, June 1994

(37) Jenny Morris 'Independent Living Project: final evaluation' Rowntree Foundation 1993

(38) Hugh Card 'Senior Citizen Advocacy' Open MIND (45), June/July 1990

(39) Frances Rickford 'Lost for Words' 7 January 1993 Social Work Today (Pges 14-15)

(40) National Association of Health Authorities and Trusts 'Investing in Patient's Representatives' 1993 (Pge 9)

(41) Pamela Holmes 'The Patient's Friend' Nursing Times, 8 May, vol 87, no 19, 1991 (Pges 16-17)

(42) For example "If you set your stall out properly, this work (with the mentally incapacitated) can be highly remunerative and lead to satisfied clients who become attached to you.' Gordon Ashton 'Acting for Persons who lack mental capacity' The Law Society's Gazette, number 44, 5 December 1990 (Pges 23-26)

(43) Jonathan Caplan in Ivan Illich *et al* 'Disabling Professions' Marion Boyars, 1977 (Pges 93-109)

(44) WHO Regional Office for Europe 'Is the law fair to the Disabled? - a European survey' 1990 (Pge viii)

(45) Bob Perske 'Unequal Justice - what can happen when persons with retardation or other developmental disabilities encounter the criminal justice system' Abingdon 1991

(46) Clare Dyer 'Law fails blacks, says top Judge' 15 October 1994 The Guardian (Pge 3)

(47) 'Otago Service and Advocacy Project for people with intellectual disabilities' New Zealand Health and Hospitals, September/October 1990 (Pge 22)

THREE: SERVICE PROFESSIONALS

'People who continue to work in the institutionalised and pro-
fessionalised structures of society . . . have a vital part to play
in the coming transformation of society. But they must decide
which side they are on. Are they working for some variant of a
hyper-expansionist, elitist, institutionalised, authoritarian
future . . . in which people like themselves will dominate other
people? Are they simply coasting along in their comparatively
privileged position? Or are they ready to commit themselves to
work for a sane, humane, ecological future? Are they prepared
to use their skills, their experience and their position to enlarge
the range of other people's autonomy? Are they prepared to
give away their own relative superiority?' (1)

The various service professionals - nurses, doctors, social workers
- have a long history of advocacy mixed in with oppressive social
control. The first social work textbook has a footnote on the
German Elberfeld system of the early 1870s stressing assessment as
a real test of genuine destitution: 'In the first place the applicant for
relief is subjected to an examination so close and searching, so
absolutely inquisitorial, that no man who could possibly escape
from it would submit to it.' (2) A very long way from advocacy!
Nevertheless, many social work commentators view it as a core
function. Siporin argues that the social worker is 'a spokesman for
the needy in our society, particularly for the poor and disadvantaged
. . . More recently, this has been referred to as the social worker's
advocacy role, although with some confusion about its place in an
adversary process, and with some neglect about the need for balance
between social obligations and the rights of both social workers and
clients'. (3) Case advocacy is defined as 'partisan intervention on
behalf of an individual client or identified client group with one or
more secondary institutions to secure or enhance a needed service,
resource or entitlement'. (4)
Jordan's argument is both more subtle and complex. 'Two powerful paradigms of the social worker have dominated the professional
image. The first is that of the counsellor - skilful, attentive, accurately empathic and accepting of the client's individuality. The second is that of the advocate, who champions the oppressed, and turns
the tables on those who exploit and exclude the client. Both these
activities are uncharacteristic of everyday social work.' (5)

Nursing commentators are much more evangelistic: '. . . nurses are in the best position to carry out the advocacy role. Nurses have knowledge of the system, alternative treatments, and other disciplines, while still being able to relate to patients on their own terms. Nurses can also relate to the management of both the patient's and society's changing needs.'(6)   Even the usually sceptical Beardshaw gets carried away on this strong tide. Apparently advocacy is 'a logical application of the planned systematic and focused care . . . which should be the goal of modern nursing'. (7)

The United Kingdom Central Council (UKCC) Code of Professional Conduct states that the nurse must 'act always in a way as to promote and safeguard the well-being and interests of patients/clients'. The implication is that 'nurses should act as advocates for their patients and clients, representing their points of view when they are unable to represent themselves'.(8)   From critical care nursing: 'Overall it seems logical that advocacy is integral with nursing, indeed as the aim of nurses working in critical care areas is to meet the needs of unconscious patients until such time that they are able to participate actively in their own health care, it would seem that advocacy in ITU (intensive treatment unit) and nursing are synonymous.' (9)

Even more fervently evangelistic: 'The role of advocate has become widely accepted in the nursing and caring services. Indeed, it is recognised in law and is central to government health care policy objectives set out in the White Paper 'Caring for People' (1991) which describes the nurse's advocacy role as "to promote and develop the right services to help people live in their own homes whenever that is possible and realistic; to ensure those who provide services prioritise carers' needs for practical support; to assess both known and unidentified needs, and to make effective and efficient care management the fundamental keystone to high quality care".' (10) Here the term 'advocacy' is used in a much wider and vaguer context, very difficult to separate from the provision of general care.

We change from evangelism to old-fashioned tub-thumping with ' . . . the opportunities and skills of advocacy are already available from CPNs (community psychiatric nurses): they are in direct contact with the client; they work in partnership with the client; they have an in depth knowledge of the individual client's personality and family and social situation, and a trusting relationship; they are aware of the wider social and environmental contexts, and they have the necessary counselling, listening and explaining skills. They also have a sound knowledge of the mental health system and the variety

30

of relevant agencies to which the client may need access, such as housing, social security and local and central government departments'. (11) According to this simplistic version, it is all straightforward as all vacant posts are filled by CPNs. No one else need apply.

Not to be left out of this suddenly popular pastime, a recent discussion paper from the Royal College of General Practitioners on older people, suggests that 'there are times when general practitioners and professional workers have to act as the patient's advocate'. But by way of contrast, the Confederation of Health Service Employees has suggested that professionals may not be 'the most appropriate people to act as advocates since they may lack the necessary time and persistence'. (12) Not surprisingly, few of these advocacy bids make any reference to possible conflicts in the various roles and functions.

CONFLICTS

It seems clear from the increasing numbers of articles in the professional press that the advocacy bandwagon is quickening. That relates, in part, to the substantial changes in the care in community field and increasing emphasis on user participation in services. It is perceived as a new and expanding area, in some ways, ready for colonisation. However, most service professionals face an essential and fundamental clash of vested interests. They have core professional obligations but also conflicting responsibilities which arise from roles as agents of their employing bodies - social services, voluntary organisations or health authorities. It still says Broadshire Social Services or NHS trust or whatever on their monthly pay cheque. Gathercole outlines five different sorts of conflict:

'**organisational;** service survival interests are often seen as more important than user interests. Scandal must be avoided, even at the cost of continuing neglect, abuse or exploitation.

professional: staff may discourage promotion of users' interests which may challenge the good name of the profession.

managerial: interests of managers may differ from what grass roots staff see as the interests of the users, e.g. bonuses paid to health service managers for resettling people from hospitals.

personal: even if serving only one person, one's own personal needs, e.g. for rest etc. may be a source of conflict.

competition: service workers have competing demands on their time from other residents.' (13)

These add up to considerable barriers for most and seem to require a Mother Theresa figure with a private income. Service professionals may try hard to represent individual users' interests in various settings like case conferences or ward rounds but, at the same time, are salaried from the service agency, often seen as the major source of oppression. For example, '. . . the bureaucratic setting in which nursing is practised means that nurses depend for their employment upon the administration of the organisation where they work, and this will inhibit them from making criticisms and publicising bad practices and low standards'. (14)

That basic conflict exists, usually in a more subtle form, in the voluntary agencies as well. Ironically, they are often perceived as the voice of the consumer although they can be bastions of Old Testament paternalism. Certainly they may function in advocating both individually and systemically, but their money comes more and more from mechanisms like joint financing for direct service provision, bringing them in conflict with vital advocacy functions. Increasingly they are major service providers. As a Director of North West MIND, I was more frequently dealing with complaints about our own MIND provision rather than about complaints of local authority services.

Put somewhat starkly this means: 'As professionals in an institutional health care system, we are involved as agents of social control, assisting doctors to maintain the stability of a social structure which itself causes disease. Such a role is evidently not compatible with that of patient advocacy. First because we are contracted in general terms to help maintain the social order of health and illness. Second, on a more subjective level, as members of the health care establishment we have a vested interest in maintaining our exclusive power as professionals, and the hegemony of the establishment on which we depend. The nearest we can come to patient advocacy is some form of benign paternalism . . .' (15)

It is difficult for most professionals to see themselves in that light as Wolfensberger stresses: '. . . many benevolent, humanistic clinicians see themselves as servants of the public, offering themselves and their services in a non-controlling fashion. They see their clients as free agents, free to reject the offered services. Their self-concept - in part due to the indoctrination received during training - is frequently compatible with action perceived as controlling, directing or dictating client behaviour. Yet here it is where so many human service workers deceive themselves, because their roles are not only almost always societally sanctioned, but in an endless array of encounters between server and the served, the server is the interpreter of, and agent for, the intents of society, and wields a truly amazing amount of power and control, even if he *[sic]* may not consciously perceive himself as so doing . . . Indeed, it is not too much to say that who will be rich or poor, healthy or sick, bright or dumb, honest or crooked - and even born or unborn - depends in many cases, and to a significant extent, upon the decision of human managers.'(16)

Rose comments on these conflicting pressures: 'Social work has been embedded in a structural contradiction since its professional origins. The nature of this contradiction arises from the social historical fact that the profession receives both its legitimation and primary funding from the capitalist state, the same structural base that creates the poverty and abuses of its clients. The profession has been able to avoid or deny its internal contradiction through the adaptation or development of individual defect explanatory paradigms to guide its practice. Whether the guiding model has been taken from psychiatry, psychodynamic theory, ego psychology, behaviourism, or even more recent progressive psychosocial concepts, the result has been the same - systematic exclusion of the social reality of capitalist structures, ideological forms and processes shaping daily life and individual subjective experience.' (17) In order to be effective advocates, we need to adopt views that are essentially projective and structuralist. We have to see the issues as embedded in social and economic structures as well as in the individual lives of our clients/patients.

With these immense pressures, it is naïve of Tschudin to warn that 'a nurse must accept that she does not do what she thinks is right by her own value system; she can only be a patient advocate when she defends the patient's values and rights not her own'. (18) In a similar vein: ' . . . substitute decision-makers should render a decision that they believe the patients would have chosen for themselves if they were competent.' (19) However righteous these various views are, they completely under-estimate the immense pressures on employees. Many services operate amid an overall atmosphere of fear and terror. Millar is more sanguine: 'The NHS has a structure which is almost military in terms of who is allowed to talk to whom and whose opinion one is allowed to value.'(20)

For individuals the risks can be very considerable: ' . . . the individual nurse who pleads the patient's cause may be ostracised by her colleagues. To stand up and be counted is always hard, the more so when it involves an implied criticism of colleagues . . . To try to be a patient's friend and advocate may be to go beyond both nursing's competence and a realistic view of the nurse-patient relationship. If this is the case, then advocacy could be one bandwagon that nursing should let pass by.' (21)

Even more sobering: 'An agency-based social worker can only bite the hand that feeds and get away with it for so long before being reprimanded, if not fired . . . empowerment of oppressed clients requires that a social worker not only act as an advocate with and on their behalf but also help them identify and change the dynamics that enable them to contribute to their own situation of oppression or to that of others.' (22) 'Rather than forgo the rewards of team membership and a close relationship with the doctor, the nurse will abdicate her patient advocate function, maintain the team's definition of a united front and accept her subordinate status within the team . . . to advocate, nurses have to drop the handmaiden image.' (23) 'The social psychological repercussions - to run the possibility of being excluded from the team, even scapegoated - are extensive.'(24)

A national nursing document implies more dilemmas. 'Advocacy is concerned with promoting and safeguarding the well-being and interests of patients and clients. It is not concerned with conflict for its own sake . . . the exercise of professional accountability involves the practitioner in assisting the patient by making such representations on behalf as he would make himself if he were able.' (25) This rather fearful reference both to conflict and the implied warning is fascinating.

The conflicts exist on many different levels. Care in the community professionals have so many other functions which conflict significantly with simply speaking out on behalf of the patient/client. For example, they have major treatment roles as well as legal responsibilities. Examine the tangle of different responsibilities in this knot: 'Health professionals have a duty when recommending certain forms of treatment to ensure patients are notified of any significant risks. This duty, however, is qualified by the power to withhold information if it is deemed to be in the patient's interest not to know. The doctrine of therapeutic privilege allows health professionals to set aside the normal duty of disclosure. Similarly, consultants have the power to withhold such data from patients who are exercising their rights under the Data Protection Act (1984) and the Access to Health Records Act (1990), as in the absence of a Bill of Rights for patients, there is no clear right in law for them to obtain this information.' (26) Now you see the advocacy function and now you don't; now we are telling people what they need to know and now we're not because in our judgement it isn't good for them! Higgs comments sardonically about psychiatry: 'No other profession sees it as their duty to suppress information simply to preserve happiness.' (27)

Further dilemmas are illustrated in this passage: 'If you are advocating on behalf of someone who is able to speak for himself, you must be very clear about his wishes before you speak on his behalf. It is also your responsibility to ensure that he has the right information on which to base his views. Occasionally, people are tempted to slant the information they supply in order to bring about the decision that they think is best for the client. This is paternalistic, the exact opposite of advocacy . . .' Curiously, further on, we get an unconscious example of this same paternalism. 'If you are pleading the case of a patient who is unable to speak for himself, you need to weigh up the evidence and decide on what **you consider to be the best**, taking into account all his needs - physical, psychological, social and emotional.' [my bold type] (28) It is not the professional deciding what is best, but the genuine attempt to get into the mind of the patient/client, which is the basis of genuine advocacy.

A splendid example of confusion: '. . . an elderly woman was extremely puzzled by her social worker's refusal to act as an advocate on her behalf in her dealing with the housing department and health professionals. The social worker felt she should be encouraged to undertake these negotiations herself as she did not want to encourage dependency, but had not shared the rationale for her actions. Instead she imposed an ideal of independence . . . which was not open to negotiation.' (29) On one level, the client was being pressurised in to self-advocacy by being denied the advocacy role of the professional service worker! On another, we are simply observing the simple reframing of old fashioned paternalism. Anyway the local government Ombudsman found in the client's favour, commenting that very little had been explained to her.

Apparently, male or female nurses should protect patients against male doctors. '. . . nurses should be prepared to speak out for the client/patient within health care at the policy making level... to counterbalance the sometimes distorted priorities claimed by the medical profession which may fail to coincide with the interests of the population in respect to health... to represent the needs of women in relation to health, since in spite of an increase of women entering medical school this is not reflected in the number of women doctors at an influential level in health care management.' (30) 'Many nurses, however, feel oppressed by doctors, so obviously the patient is likely to feel threatened to an even greater degree.' (31)   In this not so hidden agenda, it seems that patients are being used as pawns to defend nurses. This is a dubious basis for advocacy.

However, we are saved by counter dogmatism: '. . . first the role of advocate and the role of nurse are incompatible, thus making nurse advocacy impossible; second, that the drive towards advocacy is undesirable for the healthcare team and the patient; and third, that what is often described as advocacy is no more, and no less, than nurses trying to act in the best interests of their patients, a role that has always been theirs.' 'To suggest that a patient has an advocate when it is that very person who may be involved in the treatment that the patient is resisting is analogous to suggesting that the police can act as advocates for people in custody.'

They finish with a good old-fashioned broadside: '. . . advocacy may have less to do with nurses wanting to act in the best interests of their patients, and more with a power struggle between medicine and nursing.' They suggest that nurses' renewed interest is inspired by motives considerably less than pure altruism. Nurses may be using patients as pawns in a power struggle; that nurse advocacy is a new version of 'nurse knows best'; and that claiming to be advocates is simply empire building. (32) Sang, an early pioneer of British citizen advocacy commented even more fiercely : 'Professional involvement is not just inappropriate, it puts any advocacy scheme at risk. This simple message seems to run contrary to the vocational ideology of "professional advocacy".' (33)

The conflicts are not always so clear cut. There is sometimes not a clear choice between conflict or its absence but more of a long continuum. Many battles fought by nurses and social workers are **not** against the interests of the services provided by their employing agency. Social workers often represent the interests of clients battling against the monsters of social security, in which their employers are, at worst, only indirectly involved. 'A few months ago, Michael was finding life very tough. His benefit income of £61 a week was just not enough to pay his phone bill, buy a new gas fire, replace worn-out clothes and provide him with enough to eat. He had survived on benefit income for years and was not in debt, but things were piling up. He was very worried about his money and had asked for his telephone to be disconnected. He had stopped going to MIND events because he had no spending money, and he felt ashamed of his uncut hair and poor clothing.'

'When he was contacted by a mental health social worker, his loss of weight, burns from his unsafe gas fire and money worries had begun to concern his friends and relatives. Three months after this contact with the worker, Michael's income had more than doubled. This was because of the support he had received, which resulted in a successful claim for Disability Living Allowance.' (34) Professionals are struggling with private nursing homes; social security tribunals; educational authorities. . .

As I write this an academic friend with a clinical psychologist are battling against the exclusion of two 'special needs' children from mainstream education. They are 'sitting in' the entrance to Preston, Lancashire, County Hall. Their paid work in education does not conflict directly with the crusade to access mainstream education although it will not endear them to their employers.

The Police and Criminal Evidence Act 1984 provides a further example of minimal conflict. It includes safeguards for some vulnerable persons held in police custody. The relevant guidance involves some social workers and nurses in an advocacy role: 'In the case of persons who are mentally ill or mentally handicapped, it may, in certain circumstances be more satisfactory for all concerned if the "appropriate adult" is someone who has experience of training in their care rather than a relative lacking in such qualifications.' (35)

There are necessary and important tensions between the various professionals and service users. 'Users also need to be aware of professional assumptions about their needs so that these are open to negotiation. If there is no acknowledgement that professional definitions of needs may differ from user-defined needs, there is no basis for negotiation.' (36) Much discussion amongst professionals denies the need for such negotiations.

Many care professionals are extremely nervous about and resistant to external advocacy systems. They resent the outside and inside interference and become defensive. Hayward sees the claiming of unique powers of advocacy as a sort of proactive strike against possible intruders. 'It is natural for mental health professionals in hospitals and residential establishment to deny the need for advocacy. Staff frequently feel they are the advocates. This frequently leads to the well-intentioned but suffocating paternalism that pervades public services.' (37)

Some professionals see advocacy as territory over which they have major control. Outsiders are potentially hostile invaders who overtly or covertly want to undermine their position. The Family Rights Group comments relevantly: 'a serious flaw in some social workers' thinking . . . is that once they have taken a decision that opposing that judgement is deemed to be acting contrary to the best interests of the client.' (38) On a more structural level, Lipsky comments about the myth of street level bureaucrats, including social workers: 'it assumes only that policy and people who implement it are well intentioned and that their work constitutes a net social benefit.' (39) If you believe that you'll believe anything.

Part of this overall struggle between service professionals and mainly professional advocates lies in the battle for influence and power; part comes from deep philosophical differences. Just consider these in a psychiatric context: 'There is one view that a man should be protected from those who could care for him, for all are prone to abuse him. The other view suggests that patient care deals with the whole person and requires direct intervention in aspects of his life.' (40)

Service professionals, like nurses, doctors and social workers, suffer from a huge problem of vested interest. They are most frequently employed by the services complained against. Although they cannot be pure advocates, they must still have an important advocacy role. Wolfensberger outlines the different barriers to advocacy but still writes: 'Everything that has been said so far . . . does not deny that a staff member of a service agency might not be an advocate. However, in order to be an advocate, such a worker would usually have to act outside the scope of his/her agency and work role, and/or reject rather than implement its society - mandated policies - with all the risks pertaining to that.' (41) Advocates are so scarce, who else is going to speak out on an daily basis for the relatively powerless, except the service people? In those subterranean areas of services like prisons and special hospitals, who else is going to point out their deficiencies?

WHISTLEBLOWERS

The real heroes of internal advocacy are whistleblowers. (42) They can exert pressure from inside to improve often scandalous situations. 'An individual must have the right to blow the whistle on his organisation . . . rather than be forced to condone illegality . . . oppression of the disadvantaged . . .' (43) Titmuss pointed out that 'Criticism from without of professional conduct and standards of work tends to be increasingly resented the more highly these groups are organised'. (44) Attacks coming from within are seen as disloyal, particularly if made public.

One early example of whistleblowing was 'Sans Everything' published in 1967, greeted by ferocious attacks. Six nurses and two social workers courageously reported their experiences of working on geriatric wards. 'During my period as a male nursing assistant for about seven months in Comfort Hospital, and about six weeks in Cosy Hospital, I saw a great many acts of calculated cruelty and enough corruption to sicken me completely . . . The conduct of these institutions left me boggling at the thought that such massive corruption and cruelty could be tolerated in a civilised community . . . the charge nurse went into assaults armed with a short-handled sweeping brush, and laid about him indiscriminately and with great ferocity. Bruises were commonplace, split eyebrows quite frequent. If the wound had to be stitched, and the daily-occurrence book written up, it was always blamed on the assault of one patient on another.' (45)

Paul Walsh, then a senior nursing officer at Wexham Park Hospital, Slough, faced disciplinary action in 1982 for refusing to forcibly restrain a psychiatric patient who had declined to have an injection of flupenthixol at the request of a consultant. In the eyes of the 'Nursing Mirror' what was 'at stake was the whole autonomy of the nursing profession vis-à-vis medicine. If nurses do not act as advocates of patients, particularly in psychiatric hospitals, no one else will. No longer can, and should, nurses be allowed to be kicked around by doctors when they believe the doctor is wrong.' (46) Notice the old power struggle raises its head once more. Walsh was later dismissed and won the relevant action in the High Court but the health authority went to the Court of Appeal on a technicality and won. The House of Lords turned down his petition. (47)

More recently, Graham Pink, a charge nurse, spoke out against poor staffing and conditions in the Stockport psycho-geriatric services. His national nursing council supported him. A colleague drawing up a petition to support him wrote this letter to her Unit Manager: 'I know most of my colleagues agree with him on this matter but, unfortunately, many were reluctant to sign a petition fearing recriminations. It has come to my knowledge that I have already been branded a "troublemaker" for my efforts. Those signatures I already have I now feel reluctant to pass on to you for fear of further recriminations against them.' (48)

Black health visitor Desmond Smith won record damages of £27,000 against his health authority. He was racially abused by a client in the presence of colleagues. He complained but the authority preferred to look into a later complaint lodged against him by the client involved. He was dismissed in February 1992. Helped by the Health Visitors' Association to put his case, he won the damages at an industrial tribunal. (49)

Students of the various professions can be easy targets. Simon

Rundell, a student nurse in Bloomsbury Health Authority, explained what happened when he and other students complained about out-dated clinical practice: 'There were outright examples of victimisation. One nurse was declared "unsafe". I had horrendous reports, but thankfully my tutors threw them in the bin because they knew what was going on . . . Outspoken students are likely to be ear-marked as trouble-makers.' (50)

'Professionals who elect to be "whistleblowers" should expect negative criticism from colleagues, since their action inevitably threatens the stability of those remaining within the system.' (51) Persecution of whistleblowers is not confined to health and social services. Social Audit suggests that whistleblowers in industry need fresh legal protection. The company concerned would have to show that 'where the whistleblower claims unfair dismissal, the burden of proof would be on the employer to show that whistleblowing was not a factor in dismissal . . . Whistleblowers should be protected from blacklisting . . .' (52)

Beardshaw notes in the seminal study: 'Nurses have good reasons for keeping quiet about abuse in mental hospitals; silence is a nor-mal, human response to intimidation and fear. Their silence is enforced by vested interests within the hospital organisation: inter-ests which have something to hide or which prefer not to face embarrassing, painful and difficult truths . . . This enforced silence involves a denial of basic human rights. Through it, patients suffer within a "caring" environment. Through it, caring nurses are deprived of free speech and are effectively prevented from follow-ing their profession's basic tenets.' (53)

In 1993, the so called 'Whistleblowers' Charter' was launched by Virginia Bottomley, the Health Minister, to encourage more staff to report alleged malpractice. 'The code alone is not enough . . . Many hospitals do not have a culture which allows staff to raise serious concerns. There is no sense of mutual trust between the employee groups within the organisation.' (54) The recent report on mental health nursing stated the harsh realities: 'Unfortunately, nurses still face difficulties in speaking out on behalf of those most vulnerable to the negative effects of poor service provision. Users report there is a tendency for some professionals to close ranks rather than con-front bad practice. This cannot be condoned . . . Nurses should speak out on behalf of the people in their care, but sometimes should also have access to advocates on the wards or in the community, who can express their wishes and views unreservedly.' (55)

TRAINING?

It seems peculiar that although many professionals claim advocacy as an important core function none outside the law, consider it worthwhile to provide effective training. There is little discussion of the methods and or even purposes of advocacy in the various textbooks. 'Given that advocacy is part of the social work task, it is depressing that there is so little training or literature available to help social work staff develop effective advocacy skills.' (56) '. . . as patients become increasingly ill, their personal control over their own destinies may give way to intensified dependence on their physicians, and this dependence may result in poorer attention to, interest in, and recall of information about consent . . . Nurses would be better equipped to take on a nurse advocate role if they were specifically trained to do so. It is inaccurate to suggest that advocacy is part of the nurse's role, while what we are really doing is merely paying lip service to the concept'. (57) In a special hospital report, Rae asks for '. . . education for nursing staff in understanding user involvement and advocacy skills, particularly enabling self advocacy and helping patients to express their views and suggestions'. (58)

As one example of what this might involve, Bateman suggests that principled advocacy involved with the social security benefits system has various stages:

> **'the presentation of the problem**
> **information gathering**
> **legal research**
> **advising and counselling**
> **negotiation and advocacy**
> **litigation.'** (59)

He suggests a thorough and detailed training programme for social workers and others.

The best protagonist for advocacy by service professionals is Black. He wants social workers in mental health to turn away from therapeutic models - seen as part of the problem - to advocacy models, part of the solution. '. . . typical clinical models of social work inadvertently reproduce the feeling of powerlessness, the experience of oneself as inadequate, incompetent or crazy, even when adaptation to client roles may promote immediate or short-term relief and the appearance of growth'. (60)

He argues for three major elements in professional work with service users: **contextualisation, empowerment and collectivity**. 'Focusing on **contextualisation**, on bringing to consciousness both the unique experience of the individual and the social base for that individual's experience, also means that attention must be primarily given to the structural factors which impose dependency . . . **empowerment** means a process of dialogue through which the client is continuously supported to produce the range of possibility that he/she sees appropriate to his/her needs; that the client is the center for all decisions that affect her/his life . . . **collectivity** means that the focus on the social basis of identity and experience is designed to reduce isolation and the terror of experiencing oneself as uniquely defective and stagnant.' (61)

ISSUES

It is important to continue raising the considerable issues of role conflict and lack of independence within the various professions, especially where they are directly employed by service providers. Various relevant articles still express little awareness of the dilemmas that service professionals ordinarily face. For example, recently McMahon examined the role of school psychologists as child advocates without analysing any of these conflicts. (62)

It seems clear that, despite the problems of lack of independence, care professionals **must** continue to have a major advocacy role. That raises difficult problems about the serious cost to individuals in a culture where services are so defensive. Beresford cautions: 'Can professionals be advocates? Yes, but when they have power over individual service users, or responsibilities other than to speak for the person, then there is a conflict of interest, and the person will need an independent advocate. But at all times service workers need to have some awareness of, and try to protect the service user's interests (however imperfectly they do this, given conflicts of interest) and not just leave this to the advocate.' (63)

Their continuing contribution must come with much greater self-awareness. It is easy to use the process of liberation as a more sophisticated force for further imprisonment. Skynner suggests that care workers are driven people who are often vicarious clients. (64) Freire writes even more sternly: 'The oppressors, who oppress, exploit, and rape by virtue of their power, cannot find in this power the strength to liberate either the oppressed or themselves. Only the power that springs from the weakness of the oppressed will be sufficiently strong to free both. Any attempt to "soften" the power of the oppressed almost always manifests itself in the form of false generosity . . .' (65)

In a recent study, almost 90% of social workers reported involvement in advocacy as part of their job but less than 1% considered themselves full-time advocates. Most advocacy was on behalf of individuals internal to the organisation they worked for; any collective advocacy was done as volunteers. The author concludes: 'The National Association of Social Workers should explore ways to support and understand social work advocacy, and schools of social work should rededicate themselves to teaching and practising and studying this core activity.' (66)

Zola has a last and powerful word about the dilemmas which face the medical profession particularly: 'As long as the deliverers of service are markedly different in gender, economic class, and race from those to whom they offer services, as long as accessibility to medical care is a privilege rather than a right, as long as the highest income groups are health care professionals, as long as the most-profit-making enterprises include the pharmaceutical and insurance industries, society is left with the uncomfortable phenomenon of a portion of its population, living, and living well, off the sufferings of others and to some extent even unwittingly having such a vested interest in the continuing existence of such problems.'(67)

References:
(1) James Robertson in 'The Sane Alternative' Robertson 1983 (Pge 90)
(2) Quoted in Mary Richmond 'Social Diagnosis' Russell Sage Foundation 1917 (Pge 28)
(3) Max Siporin 'Introduction to Social Work Practice' Collier MacMillan 1975
(4) B.G. McGowan 'Advocacy' in the Encyclopaedia of Social Work, 18th edition, National Association of Social Workers, 1987 (Pge 92)
(5) Bill Jordan 'Counselling, Advocacy and Negotiation' British Journal of Social Work vol 17 No 2, April 1987, (Pges 135-146)
(6) Agnes Graham 'Advocacy: what the future holds' British Journal of Nursing: 1992, vol. 1 No 3 (Pges 148-150)
(7) V. Beardshaw 'Conscientious Objectors at Work' Social Audit 1981
(8) Julie-Ann Sutor 'Can Nurses be effective advocates?' Nursing Standard 17 February 1993
(9) J.W. Albarran 'Advocacy in Critical Care - an evaluation of the implications for nurses and the future' Intrusive and Critical Care Nursing: 8: 1992, (Pges 47-53)
(10) Ann Long and Patrick McGreevy 'Advocating Advocacy' Community Psychiatric Nursing Journal, (October 1993 (Pge 10)
(11) Ibid. (Pge 12)
(12) Quoted in Alison Wertheimer 'Speaking Out: citizen advocacy and older people' Centre for Policy on Ageing 1993 (Pge 36)

(13) Quoted in Kate Butler *et al* 'Citizen Advocacy - a powerful partnership' National Citizen Advocacy 1988 (Pge 13)

(14) Christine Webb 'Speaking Up for Advocacy' Nursing Times, August 26, Vol. 83, No 34, 1987 (Pges 33-35)

(15) Sam Porter 'Siding with the System' Nursing Times, 12 October, Vol 84 No 41, 1988

(16) Wolf Wolfensberger 'The Principle of Normalisation in Human Services' NIMR 1972

(17) Stephen Rose 'Advocacy/Empowerment: an approach to clinical practice for Social Work' Journal of Sociology and Social Welfare, Vol 17, June 1990 (Pges 41-51)

(18) V Tschudin 'Ethics in Nursing' (2nd edition) Butterworth Heinemann, 1992

(19) William J Winslade *et al.* 'Making Medical Decisions for the Alzheimer's Patient: Paternalism and Advocacy' Psychiatric Annals, 14, 3 March 1984

(20) Barbara Millar 'The Call of the Wild' Health Service Journal, 10 November 1993

(21) Kath Melia 'Whose side are you on?' Vol 83 No 29, Nursing Times July 22, 1987 (Pges 46-8)

(22) Maurice J. Moreau 'Empowerment through Advocacy and Consciousness-Raising: implications of a structural approach to social work' Journal of Sociology and Social Welfare, Vol 17, (Pges 53-67), 1990

(23) B.J. Kalisch 'Of half gods and mortals: Aesculapian authority' Nursing Outlook 23:1; 1975

(24) Chapter 7 in David Brandon 'Innovation without Change? - consumer power in psychiatric services' MacMillan 1990

(25) United Kingdom Central Council for Nursing, Midwifery and Health Visiting 'Exercising accountability' 1989

(26) Issues in Nursing 'Patient Advocacy' Professional Nurse, March 1994

(27) Roger Higgs in Michael Lockwood (ed) 'Moral Dilemmas in Modern Medicine' Oxford University, 1985 (Pge 102)

(28) 'The How of Advocacy' David Carpenter Nursing Times: 1 July Vol 88 No 27, 1992

(29) Margaret Clarke 'Patient/Client Advocates' Journal of Advanced Nursing, 1989, 14, (Ppges 513-14)

(30) Anna Coote 'Charter Blight' Social Work Today 12 November 1992 (Pges 14-15)

(31) Judith Sawyer 'On Behalf of the Patient': Nursing Times, 12 October 1988: Vol 84 No 41, (Pge 28)

(32) Peter Allmark and Robin Klarzynski 'The Case against Nurse Advocacy' British Journal of Nursing, 1992, Vol. 2 No 1 (Pges 33-36)

(33) Bob Sang in Anny Brackx and Catherine Grimshaw (Eds) 'Mental Health in Crisis' Pluto Press 1989

(34) Ann Davis 'Claiming Success' Open MIND December 1993

(35) Alan Skelt 'Held in Police Custody' Nursing Times, Vol 84 No 4, 1988 (Pges 50-52)

(36) Nina Biehal 'Participation, Rights and Community Care' British Journal of Social Work, 1993, 23, (Pges 443-458)

(37) Robert Hayward 'Developing an Advocacy Service for People with Mental Health Problems in Bradford' Report of the conference held at the Community Arts Centre on 9 November, 1991

(38) Barclay Report 'Social Workers - their roles and tasks' Bedford Square Press 1981

(39) Michael Lipsky 'Street level Bureaucracy - Dilemmas of the individual in Public Services' Sage 1980

(40) Wolf Wolfensberger 'A Multi-component advocacy/protection Schema' CAMR 1977,

(41) Ibid. (Pge 24)

(42) Philip Bean 'Mental Disorder and Legal Control' Cambridge University Press, 1986

(43) Franklin D. Chu and Sharland Trotter 'The Madness Establishment' Ralph Nader Study Group on the National Institute of Mental Health, Grossman 1974

(44) Richard Titmuss 'Essays on the Welfare State' Allen & Unwin 1958, (Pge 127)

(45) Barbara Robb 'Sans Everything: a case to answer' Nelson 1967 (Pges 43-44)

(46) See Mark Allen's editorial: 'The Start of a New Campaign' Nursing Mirror, 15 September 1982 (Pge 7) and Cherill Hicks 'Why I am opposing the Doctors' Nursing Times, 22 September, 1982 (Pges 1579-80)

(47) Paul Walsh 'Speaking up for the Patient' Nursing Times, 1 May 1985 (Pges 24-26)

(48) David Brindle 'The Resounding Call of the Whistle-Blower Nurse' The Guardian, 4 July 1990

(49) Peter Baddeley 'Health Visitor wins case' The Whistle No 2, May 1993 (Pge 3)

(50) Amanda Tattam 'Blowing the Whistle' Nursing Times, June 7, Vol 85 No 23, 1989 (Pge 20)

(51) Steve Baldwin and Phil Barker (Eds) 'Ethical Issues in Mental Health' Chapman & Hall 1991 (Pge 185)

(52) Marlene Winfield 'Minding your own Business - self regulation and whistleblowing in British companies' Social Audit 1990

(53) Virginia Beardshaw 'Conscientious Objectors at Work - Mental Hospital Nurses - a Case Study' Social Audit, 1981 (Pge 81)

(54) Barbara Millar 'The Call of the Wild' Health Service Journal, 18 November 1993

(55) 'Working in Partnership - a collaborative approach to Care' Report of the Mental Health Nursing Review Team HMSO (Pges 14-15) 1994

(56) Neil Bateman 'Legal Lessons;' Social Work Today: 1 August 1991

(57) Annette Morrison 'The nurse's role in relation to advocacy' Nursing Standard, 3 July 1991

(58) Malcolm Rae 'Freedom to Care - Achieving Change in culture and nursing practice in a mental health service' Ashworth Hospital 1993

(59) Neil Bateman 'Legal Lessons' Social Work Today: 1 August 1991

(60) Stephen Rose 'Advocacy/Empowerment: an approach to clinical practice for Social Work' Journal of Sociology and Social Welfare, Vol 17, June 1990 (Pge 45)

(61) Ibid. (Pges 48-9) and see also Stephen Rose and Bruce Black 'Advocacy and Empowerment - Mental Health - care in the community' Routledge & Kegan Paul, 1985

(62) Thomas J. McMahon 'On the Concept of Child Advocacy: a review of the theory and methodology' School Psychology Review, Vol 22 No 4, 1993 (Pges 744-755)

(63) Peter Beresford 'Advocacy' in 'Speaking Out for Advocacy - a report of the National Conference' Labyrinth 1994

(64) Robin Skynner 'Institutes and how to survive them - mental health training and consultation' Tavistock/Routledge 1989 (Pge 158)

(65) Paulo Freire 'The Pedagogy of the Oppressed' Penguin Education 1972 (Pge 21) and in his 'Cultural Action for Freedom' Penguin Education 1972, he defines conscientization as 'the process in which men, not as recipients, but as knowing subjects, achieve a deepening awareness both of the socio-cultural reality which shapes their lives and of their capacity to transform that reality'. (footnote Pge 51)

(66) Mark Ezell 'Advocacy Practice of Social Workers' Families in Society 'The Journal of Contemporary Human Services Families International 1994 (Pges 36-46)

(67) Irving Zola 'Healthism and Disabling Medicalization' in Ivan Illich et al 'Disabling Professions' Marion Caldars, 1977 (Pges 41-67)

FOUR: ADVOCACY BY FAMILIES

*'Treat us as partners. Remember that we have valuable opin-
ions too. Don't put us on trial. If you find our children difficult,
remember we may do the same. We would like to work with
you, but we resent being made to feel inferior when we really
have tried.'*

Philippa Russell, from a workshop in Sheffield,
Council for Disabled Children, 1994

SPEAKING OUT

Advocacy by relatives isn't just about dealing with interminable
services and professionals. It involves all the daily life issues: the
joys and sorrows; the sleeping in hourly naps; the nights of patience;
the constant renewal of optimism; all the love in action. I knew one
woman with a disabled son who had over 500 visiting cards from
social workers, nurses, psychologists in a big coffee jar. (1)

'I have two relatives needing care - one has dementia, one has
severe learning difficulties. Both have social workers (I don't).
Both social workers talk a lot about personal autonomy; the dignity
of risk; ordinary lives. But they don't realise that my life is anything
but ordinary; no time off; no sleep; no money. No paid worker
would accept my life . . . but I have to (and my mother and son suffer
as a consequence). I don't actually want much. I do need some day
care. I am now 65 and I have painful arthritis. I can no longer drive
easily. But the social workers are always suggesting activities
which require me getting up early to drive one of my relatives miles;
dashing back; dashing out again. No one has ever asked me if I
would like to go on a college course; go to the cinema, learn to
swim.' (2)

This quote reminds us that families get no training or payment and
bring considerable concerns, intimacy and passions to the process of
representation as well as despair and exhaustion. Often they are
uniquely qualified and involved to make strong cases. Families with
disabled members, particularly when their children are young, have
an unusually high degree of contact with the various professionals
and sometimes a profound knowledge of services. (3)

Lowell Weicker, a United States senator from Connecticut, who
has a son with Down's Syndrome, wrote: 'To say for our children
what they would say if they had access to power - that is our responsibility as parents. We have an obligation to repair and strengthen
the bridges Congress has built to bring disabled Americans into the

47

mainstream of life. Those who would bomb those bridges must be stopped by astute political organizing and grassroots action at the local and national level'. (4) He makes elegant and passionate connections between families and collective advocacy.

Dr Tim Hunt, head of the Cambridge Hospice, talking of his father's terminal illness: 'I think I practised what I preach. He was ill. He had a stroke. I carried him up to bed. I actually spoke to him like this. I said, "You've had a small stroke. You've lost your voice but there's a good chance of recovery". The GP wanted to send him to hospital. I said to myself Tim, here we have someone of 86 who's led a very active life and who couldn't stand to be in hospital. There's a high chance he will have another stroke. That night I went to see another patient. At seven o'clock the next morning, I went back to the house. My mother had her arms around him. He had died in his sleep.'(5)

One mother of a disabled son, described positive responses to speaking out: 'We found that when we spoke up [on behalf of Aaron], people responded to our needs. Our families generously supported us. A public health nurse and county social worker reached in with valuable information and advocacy, helping us set up daily nursing services for Aaron in our home. Scores of medical professionals offered their expertise, some of them waiving their fees, many doing much more than what their roles required. Teachers and therapists stepped in with encouragement to build on Aaron's slowly developing plans.' (6)

Arlene Schouter in Canada advocated for her disabled daughter Natalie and tackled the Premier of British Columbia, after many fruitless letters and phone calls. 'Things got even worse. Natalie was in a wheelchair. She couldn't express herself. We couldn't understand her. She got more and more frustrated with more tantrums. She was like a timebomb waiting to go off . . . I heard that the Premier was speaking at a school in Surrey about fifty miles away, two days before the election. I went early with my sister and got inside the school gym. It was a campaign rally . . . The Premier came in surrounded by bodyguards. I rushed and grabbed his arm and told him: "I am the woman who has been trying to contact you." He knew who I was. We were surrounded by the media. I'm not like this normally. I'm quiet. He handed me over to his wife. Mother to mother. She passed me over to one his Managers . . .

I sat wondering My God - what am I going to do? It was the most critical point. We were running out of time, the meeting would soon be over. I stood up and started screaming my head off. I yelled "You

promised to help my daughter. You haven't made a commitment . . .
My daughter's dying. Do something about my daughter. Is there no
help for a thirteen year old girl. . . ?" The Premier stopped his
speech and talked to me: "I will help you, no matter what it takes
even if I have to re-mortgage my own home, I will help you and your
daughter." All this was recorded on the T.V. cameras and the radio
mikes.' (7) Arlene's direct intervention was not only courageous but
extremely effective. She broke through some serious obstacles and
eventually got a tailor made service for Natalie.

DILEMMAS

Some relatives may have very different, even contrary, interests
from their disabled members. They have hidden agendas which pull
them away from just speaking on behalf of their children or parents.
It is often hard to balance competing responsibilities. There can be
tensions between self-advocacy and family-advocacy. Imagine the
decisions your parents, sisters or brothers might make about your
life, if you were unable to make them yourself! Families can be a
source of oppression, depending on the sorts of relationships people
have developed and their understanding of the meaning of disability.
Sandra Kaufman writes of her disabled daughter: 'We postpone
taking the steps that will help our children leave the nest. When they
finally make the break and are living independently, we judge and
control their actions: we make decisions about whom they can see
and date; we insist they live in "safe" neighbourhoods; we refuse to
accept that they are competent enough to make decisions about what
foods to eat, or how clean their living quarters should be; or whether
they should ride a moped, or drive a car. We reject out of hand such
adult activities as drinking, smoking, and watching X-rated movies.'
(8) She is talking about the urge to protect 'children' against the
complexities of life. She doesn't sound so different, except in
degree, from the way my own mother used to speak. She used to
press me to wear a cardigan before crossing the road to buy a newspaper - at thirty five years old !
Advocacy by families may become increasingly challenged as
more and more people with disabilities demand the right to speak for
themselves rather than relying on others, especially on issues where
parents and children ordinarily have conflicts. 'The process of
growing up implies that more and more self-determination will
replace parent guidance and that conflicts will result from this
process. Must parent advocacy be replaced by self-advocacy if
maturity is to be achieved . . .? Some families impose their plans

and opinions on the disabled family member because they feel they know best.' (9)

Some families can get hooked into the disabled family syndrome. Take the parent with a son in a mental handicap hospital, writing bitterly in the local newspaper about planned resettlement: 'How can they turn these poor defenceless innocents out into our cruel, uncaring world?' She has her son be the child in herself, the carrier of her own fearfulness about life. (10) It can be seductive to get into the 'my child as burden/victim' syndrome and define oneself as rescuer and protector. Having a disabled child can become a major element of personal and family identity. At Mencap meetings I have sometimes heard families compete as to whose child is the most disabled. "My daughter is more handicapped than your son."

Where the son or daughter has learning difficulties, there can be a problem of misguided familial benevolence. This involves doing things for children which are not necessary. Some sorts of help are age inappropriate and actually encourage a destructive dependence. This may lead to massive problems for the child growing up. The young disabled teenager may lose the struggle for independence, especially when he or she does not have the backing of a peer group. The family then takes care of the adult child who becomes passive and adjusted to disability. Any continuing struggles can easily be classified as 'challenging behaviour' and dealt with through the intervention of various professionals.

At the most acute end of these difficulties are sexuality issues. 'Joe will never marry. What kind of woman would be willing to take care of him? There's no reason to stir up this hope in the "Family Life" class just to have his heart broken. Let him take the music appreciation' (Joe's mother). (11) Sexuality highlights these dilemmas. People with learning difficulties are at high risk of sexual abuse so parents do have genuine grounds for concern. There is a very difficult balance to strike between protection and suffocation. Russell points out that a lot of people with learning difficulties don't have friends and 'the lack of experience of friendships is a poor prelude for a happy sexual life'. (12)

It is difficult for a great many parents to accept their son or daughter as a sexual being; that goes double and treble when the teenager has a disability. Brown and Turk take a somewhat partisan view: 'Parents have always been more cautious and protective about advocating sexual rights; anxious that sexual expression might lead to rejection or exploitation. They realise that stating people's rights, in isolation from responsibilities, is naïve and simplistic.

Their experiences of talking to staff have tended to perpetuate polarisation rather than create common understandings, in that staff are often unwilling to acknowledge the tenuous acceptance which is extended to them and to their adult sons or daughters by members of the public.' (13)

The same problem expressed with rather more insight: 'There is the emotional side of you which loves your child dearly and you don't want to part with him. There is the other side, common sense, which says now is the time, if you love him let him go, you are doing it for him. But there is a selfish side too, can I manage on my own? I am going to be so lonely. (Mother of Martin, aged 24)' (14) This expresses eloquently the competing drives of protection and liberation.

'I can't walk away. I do want my son to be an ordinary adult and I would welcome his friends. But sexuality? Somehow they [the social services department] talk about sexuality as if it was like getting a cheque book. They don't put it in context. What really horrified me was that on the one hand they were telling us parents not to be stuffy and to accept sex education for our children. But on the other hand, there were two years of sexual abuse in the day centre's toilets which no-one would listen to me about - my son didn't want to go in after six months and no-one believed us that something was really wrong. When they found out we were speaking the truth, there were no apologies . . . I know it happens, you can't protect everyone, but why couldn't they see that there are two sides to sexuality like everything else and it's us parents who have to pick up the pieces?' (15)

My work as a care planner/advocate with Judith and her mother Wilma in Northumberland highlighted some of these difficulties. We were wrestling with a complex labyrinth of services, involving more than fifty professionals - from incontinence advisors to social workers, from teachers to residential staff. Judith was multiply disabled and unable to speak, so I moved in to the residential home where she lived to get a better sense of what she needed and what was happening to her. In this service, she was done to rather than involved in the doing.

My primary work was with Wilma. Since her husband's death several years earlier, it seemed that her whole life revolved around her daughter who was then nineteen. To achieve increased independence for Judith meant exploring their intimate relationship. If Judith lived increasingly away from home, relied on others more her own age, what would happen to her Wilma? Where would she get the help to make the separation? The only way that she could get some of her needs met was through her disabled daughter. It was the only method of getting attention. (16)

One study of parents of children with learning difficulties suggests that there is a surprisingly low level of involvement by professionals in the vital teenage period. 'These parents were receiving little or no support to help them through the transition inherent in re-negotiating their relationship with the young people and redefining their own future. As a result, although the young people were often beginning to develop limited measures of independence, many aspects of their lives remained relatively unchanged because little was changing within their family.' (17)

In the mental health field, families and their organisations are often perceived by their relatives as more overtly oppressive . 'The family movement in the United States has grown fast and has so much credibility because they are middle-class respectable people and they are not mentally ill. The family movement puts total reliance in the medical model, particularly genetics. There is this new drug out and they're volunteering their kids, who are usually mature adults, to try it out. On an individual level I can understand families have been through a lot and suffered a lot and have their own issues. I wish they would stay organised as a support group around their issues but they don't. They see themselves as representing the consumers because "we speak for people who can't speak for themselves".' (18) Families can conspire with the professionals to control their child/parent as a lifelong patient. The interests of carers and service users can become increasingly divergent.

When my father-in-law developed Alzheimer's Syndrome, we were concerned primarily with our interests rather than his. We pushed firmly for the admission to hospital because of his extremely negative effect on our family life. This was not in his best interests but was certainly in ours. He exchanged his own flat to share a noisy dormitory with twenty bewildered others. Pressing for a better deal within the hospital and also later - within the elderly severely mental ill unit - became difficult. Both my wife and I felt very guilty. The flames of those negative feelings were often fanned by staff. A charge nurse responded to our complaints about the hospital conditions: 'If you don't like it here, you can always take him home.' He knocked the scab off our guilt. (19)

At a much more complex level, the parents of Tony Bland, who sustained irreversible brain damage at the Hillsborough football disaster in 1989, pressed for his tube feeding to be stopped, so he could die. They wrote letters to the Government and went to the courts to further their campaign. Eventually, the courts agreed to the discontinuing of his tube feeding and soon afterwards he died with dignity. His father said: "As parents we should be able to have the opportunity to do what we think is best for our son". (20) But whose 'best' interests were they talking about? Certainly, they were advocating - but on whose behalf? They seemed to be drowning in a huge ocean of pain and sorrow.

OPCS estimates that by 'excluding standard child-care, some 6.8 million people in Great Britain are involved in providing informal care for others'. (21) The great majority of these are relatives. They can become isolated and feel powerlessness. ' . . . many of those providing extensive care do so over a long period without much chance of respite, sometimes with their sleep patterns being systematically disrupted by night-time demands. This and the constancy of their caring responsibilities can leave some carers with little time or energy for sustaining other interests and activities. Caring comes to be the major focus of their lives, dominating their sense of self as well as their lifestyle'. (22) As in Wilma's situation, there can be a form of symbiosis - leading to a failure to differentiate effectively between the disabled member and the rest of the family.

TRAINING

Munro in a valuable and practical paper outlines a 'step approach model' for effective advocacy by families which can gradually develop in intensity.

---

1. clearly define your objectives
2. develop a simple strategy: practice what you are going to say at home
3. implement that strategy
4. if no positive response, go further up the ladder
5. mobilise support for your 'cause'
6. if no success, go still further up the ladder; for example, raising the issue with politicians
7. pursue available legal options
8. involve the mass media
100. use civil disobedience or other extreme but non-violent methods (23)

Set up in January 1985, the Parents Involved Network Project (PIN) in south eastern Pennsylvania, USA, recruits and serves parents of children diagnosed as having serious emotional disturbances.

It started as a self-help group and later developed into case advocacy for parents, looking at the needs of children with mental health problems. 'Parents struggle to become their child's advocate - often learning how to make the systems respond to their needs by a trial-and-error process. More often than not, parents whose children have serious emotional problems are still looked upon as having caused their child's problems rather than as being the most important resource for their child. Many parents become overwhelmed, frustrated and emotionally drained by the process. Many just give up!'

'Our training focuses on the immediate needs of parents whose children have serious emotional problems.' These parents wanted more knowledge about: relevant legislation; community resources; diagnostic and treatment information; skill building.

'Group members state that having an advocate partner in attendance at the various review meetings is a valuable asset "providing them with support which helps them handle a complicated situation more easily . . ." After the meeting the parent and advocate partner can evaluate the outcome together and plan further action.' (24)

In Seattle, two parents of disabled children decided to produce a manual on ways to obtain services. They met with such resistance from the various agencies that their plans were crushed, so they set up 'The Troubleshooters'. Nowadays parents with disabled children, after sophisticated training, man telephones in twenty-four offices all over the State of Washington. 'By telephone, they train "parents in crisis" to become good self-advocates, guiding them step by step through bureaucratic mazes. At the same time they scrutinise the agencies for barriers that stand in the way. Their motto: "God helps those who help themselves. But the system helps those who know the system".' (25)

This parental pressure helps professionals to change. They need to move away from the traditional pedagogic models which emphasise their power and expertise. The 'Consumer Model' involves the teachers of disabled children seeing both children and the parents as consumers of services. 'This means that parents are seen as having the right to decide and select what they believe is best for their child and family circumstances . . . The teacher is responsible for providing parents with information and a range of options from which they can make informed choices." (26) This model recognises the potential power of parents which has consequences for collective advocacy as well. 'In times of dwindling public resources, it is especially important that parents be advocates in seeking services for their children. Lobbying efforts by parents are often helpful in preventing planned cuts in funding, or in seeking increases in funding to provide adequate programming.'

This sounds a lot like exploitation and co-option. (27)

Wout Hardeman describes the Dutch family councils in psychiatric hospitals where families make representations on behalf of their in-patient relatives. They have pressed senior management in a variety of formal and informal settings for better visiting arrangements, improved clothing and specifically for improved dental facilities. They are like a politicised form of hospital leagues of friends, influencing hospital policies. They may also represent patients who are not their relatives but occupy the same wards. (28)

Kenn Jupp provides good concrete advice for parent advocates: He suggests asking a series of searching questions about their children with disabilities:

'Are they having as full a life as other people?
In what ways are they losing out?
Do they have what other people take for granted?
Do they have equal opportunity?
Do they have as much choice as they could?
Do they have as large a repertoire of skills and concepts as they could?
Do all their friends and acquaintances have a disability?
Do others of a similar age who live locally even know they exist?
How many real friends do they have?
Do they have genuine interests and hobbies which they can pursue?
Do they only belong to clubs which are specially designed for those who are disabled?' (29)

In a way, these questions need also to be asked of the family members who are not disabled. Life can be extremely constricting for carers too. Their caring can lead them to feel isolated and socially excluded.

Jupp advises against angry gambits. 'Whether you are attending a meeting or arranging an informal contact, it is rarely worth going in with all guns blazing. No matter how angry you may feel about the situation, make certain that you check your facts with the person first. Ask general questions about what is happening and why . . . Attacks, anyway, only usually serve to put people on the defensive, which means that they are less likely to keep you fully informed of all they already know. They will also probably become antagonistic towards you - if not to your face, then when you are no longer there. Whenever they become the butt of other people's frustrated anger, bureaucrats will tend to blame you, the victim, rather than acknowledge any failure within the system.' (30)

'Don't be surprised if professionals try to put you down. Remember, no matter how nicely you put it, there will be those bureaucrats for whom you will be posing problems, who will see you as a nuisance. Therefore you may well be hit with phrases like "That's rather unreasonable you know?"" or "Don't you think you are being unrealistic?"' (31) Perske suggests that instead of becoming angry, develop 'an almost childlike questioning of the professionals (Why does he do that? What causes him to do it? Can you explain to me in words I can understand?) Do not stop until you understand the real barriers to the development of your son and daughter' (32)

Assertion training is important as a backbone for advocacy, especially in dealing with professionals. Families need to learn to be firm rather than angry; to be persistent rather than militant - until the former doesn't work! (33) Modelling relevant situations through role play; sharing different experiences can be very effective in the training. Sympathetic professionals can help but they need small egos.

PROFESSIONALS

The Local Government Ombudsman reports on a complaint made against Kent County Council by the mother of a quadriplegic daughter. He found the local authority at fault. '. . . it had significantly failed to meet the child's special educational needs. The Council had never reviewed the educational statement issued in 1986 when the child started school and, although she could not speak, her communication needs had not been determined. The Council has not shared its information with her mother, **who was regarded as an adversary rather than a partner.** Furthermore neither the old statement or the new drafts complied with the guidance issued by the Department of Education and Science, and the latest draft contained conflicting advice'. (34)

In stark contrast, co-operation between families and professionals can be extremely effective especially in collective advocacy. 'Parents and professionals had come as partners to the state capital at Lincoln from places like Norfolk, Hastings, Scottsbluff, Ogallala, and Omaha.' They had delivered a "double whammy", to state government. Parents spoke in hearings and approached legislators in the foyer. They spoke clearly about the problems people with handicaps faced in Nebraska. And, of course, legislators - being used to such people - knew how to listen respectfully, thank them for coming, and quietly shrug it off a few minutes later. But no sooner did the parents finish than their sidekicks - the professionals - took over, providing the lawmakers with detailed statistics. 'It was obvious to everyone that neither the parents nor the professionals alone could have influenced the government so powerfully. It was their well-planned, carefully detailed teamwork that did it. Many senators expressed amazement at the effectiveness of that. Said one, reminiscing at a later date, "You people were too much. If we could have kept you apart it would have been OK. But when you came at us together . . . well you were too much".' (35)

Many professionals feel threatened by family advocacy. It can be seen as loaded cannon waiting to go off. Families may ask searching questions about the professional's own training, competence and knowledge base. It could mean having to accept parents as equals. Parents can by-pass the usual formal bureaucratic channels and reach and influence senior managers and elected councillors, often speaking with passion and relevance on behalf of their children. (36)

Richardson *et al.* argue rather hopefully: 'True partnership will stem from recognition . . . With due recognition, carers will be treated as equals, given information and support and consulted in the course of service planning and delivery. With recognition, they will be treated as people to work with, to whom practical problems and hitches can be explained. Most of all, with recognition, they will have their responses to both problems and services taken seriously.' (37)

On a systems level, some voluntary organisations are moving back to advocacy and away from direct service provision. Roos noted that 'the function of parent groups has gradually shifted away from direct provision of services to handicapped children themselves to increasing emphasis in such areas as public education, governmental affairs, advocacy, and litigation'. (38) For example, the Royal National Institute for the Blind (RNIB) is offering parents of blind or partially sighted children an advocacy service. 'It aims to ensure that parents' views are taken into account when decisions are made about school provision and support for visually impaired children.' That can involve bolstering parental advocacy by accompanying them to formal meetings. (39)

Rather like Munro, Turnbull suggests a number of useful stages for families who have children with learning disabilities to deal with existing services. Beginning the process means 'remaining attuned to your son or daughters preferences, because they cannot usually communicate their own frustrations to the services'. 'Try to identify what the problem is.' 'Use brainstorming: thinking of as many solutions to the problem as possible.' 'Communicate what you decide to others.' 'Take action: it is usually necessary to combine with others and to be firm and even tempered but willing to "play hard ball" if necessary.' 'Evaluate the outcome of the action.' (40) This rather calculated process seems to professionalise parents when their major strengths - of love, intimate and detailed knowledge and passion - usually lie elsewhere.

ISSUES

Families have their own and different agendas. My best guess is that my father-in-law's would have been very different from mine. The history of the intervention of family inspired organisations, like our own Royal Mencap, has been mixed. They have pressed for caution and safety, being frequently conservative by nature. Parent-led organisations like Rescare in the learning difficulties field and the National Schizophrenia Fellowship have actively opposed the development of care in the community and pressed misguidedly for improved institutions. A study of two psychiatric wards in Scotland, showed some similarities in the top criteria for a good service between relatives and patients but also some clear differences. 'Patients were much more focused on the management of care - privacy and dignity; personal grooming etc. Relatives emphasised resource-related criteria like safe and appropriate aids, more nurses, physiotherapy . . .' (41)

Parents don't know what it's really like from the disabled person's perspective. They experience the oppression indirectly because they are usually able-bodied. (42) They are indirect consumers and their children often lack positive role models. Able-bodied parents have real problems in trying to equip their disabled child with the skills necessary to survive the hostilities of a discriminating society, let alone having the confidence to explore their ambitions and 'to go for it'. There is a strong temptation to strive to make them in your own image - able-bodied. (43)

Families can undermine self-advocacy in sophisticated ways and become a source of largely unintended and sometimes unconscious oppression. The adult children of those who are frail and elderly; the parents of those with disabilities can effectively take over the decision making; be perceived as the real experts by the various professionals. (44) This can result in considerable tensions between staff striving for the independence of people with disabilities and protective families.

We know very little about the situation of ethnic minority carers. One study showed that Afro-Caribbean, Asian and Vietnamese/Chinese carers are taking the main responsibility for the care of elderly relatives, looking after them over long hours and undertaking all the personal and household tasks. 'They are doing this at considerable costs to themselves . . . Services that do exist are not adequately meeting their needs. All carers needed more practical help in the home to enable them to provide the best possible care . . . There is no evidence that services understand the needs of carers in minority ethnic communities.' (45)

MIND raises the problems of relatives acting as interpreters for family members from minority ethnic groups. It states rather dogmatically that 'the use of family members, friends and untrained staff as interpreters is unacceptable. For example, the parents may withhold distressing information if their child is acting as interpreter. Untrained interpreters may not be familiar with mental health terminology'. (46) Surely the disabled person must make some choices about who does what in communicating his or her wishes to professionals? Interpreters who are strangers can raise just as many difficulties as those who are not.

How do we reduce the considerable resistances of professionals? The mother of a child with physical disabilities reports: 'The first words the education officer said to my husband were, "You listen to what I have to say. I'm sitting here in a suit, you are only wearing jeans. I have been in this job for many years and you have only been a parent for a few years. I don't want to hear any more of your lies or your son's lies. It's all in your imaginations."' (47) Perhaps she should go with her lawyer to the next meeting. It is not uncommon for complaints about principles to be met with personal abuse.

Twigg suggests that service providers see carers in several different ways:-

* as a resource to be exploited
* as partners in providing care
* as clients in their own right
* as a barrier to independent living (48)

All of these and other dimensions need detailed exploration. Underlying assumptions and values require analysis which should be based on open dialogue and reciprocal exploration.

Is it possible or even desirable to train families with disabled members to be more effective in their advocacy? Essentially that would involve more awareness of the existing services and increased expectations of what is possible. 'On the whole carers have fairly low hopes and expectations about help and services.'(49) People often feel devalued and deskilled. The responsibilities of caring can be heavy and exhausting. The family can feel guilty about asking for more help, especially when they are older. Advocacy can sometimes pull a parent into a semi-professional staffing position.

Changes in community care legislation seem to promise a greater role. Two crucial themes run through the relevant government guidelines: taking account of the needs of carers and not only the person with disability but practical support for the carers should have a higher priority with both the purchasers and providers of services. Until now, as we in the Brandon family learned to our cost, the only way for relatives to get some attention was through the disabled member.

References

(1) My thanks to David Wetherow from Canada, via Compuserve, for reminding me of 'love in action' and saving me from some of the worst excesses of English academia

(2) Quoted in a personal communication from Philippa Russell, 9 October1994

(3) Elizabeth Byrne, Cliff Cunningham and Patricia Sloper 'Families and their Children with Down's Syndrome: one feature in common' Routledge 1988 - point that the more disabled the child the greater that contact with professionals. (Pge 141)

(4) L. Weicker 'Sonny and Public Policy' in H.R. Turnbull and A. P. Turnbull (Editors) 'Parents Speak Out: Then and Now' (p 286) Charles E. Merrill, 1985

(5) Robert McCrum 'The Crying, Dying Game' The Guardian, 30 December 1993 (Pges 10-11)

(6) Krista Westerndorp 'One Mother's Perspective' Focus on Families, Family Support Institute, Vancouver, British Columbia, Canada, Spring 1993 (Pge 7)

(7) Taken from David Brandon's 'Direct Power' Tao, 1991 (Pges 17-18)

(8) G. Knott 'Attitudes and needs of parents of cerebral palsied children' Rehabilitative Literature, 1979, 40 (pges 190-195)

(9) Sandra Z. Kaufman 'Retarded isn't stupid, Mom' Paul Brookes, 1988 (Pge 208)

(10) Steve Dowson 'Roles and Role Players' Community Living, July 1993 (Pge 13)

(11) Susan M. Daniels 'From parent-advocacy to self-advocacy: a problem of transition' Exceptional Education Quarterly, vol 3, 1982 (pges 25-32)

(12) Philippa Russell Personal Communication 9 October 1994

(13) Hilary Brown and Vicky Turk 'Sexuality: towards a more balanced view' in Nick Bouras (Editor) 'Mental Health in Mental Retardation - recent advances and practice' Cambridge University Press: 1994

(14) Ann Richardson and Jane Ritchie 'Letting Go - dilemmas for parents whose son or daughter has a mental handicap' Open University Press 1989 (pge 80)

(15) Quoted in Philippa Russell Personal Communication 9 October 1994

(16) For more on Wilma and Judith see David Brandon 'The Yin and Yang of Care Planning' Anglia Polytechnic University, 1993

(17) Further Education Unit 'Self-Advocacy and Parents - the impact of self-advocacy on the parents of young people with disabilities' FEU 1989 (Pges 34-35)

(18) Quoted in Mary O'Hagan 'Stopovers: on my way home from Mars' Survivors Speak Out, 1993 (Pge 35)

(19) David Brandon 'Living with Ernie' MIND OUT May/June 1979 and more recently with Ray Jack 'Struggling with Services' chapter 13 in Ian J. Norman and Sally Redfern (editors) 'Mental Health Care of Elderly People' Churchill Livingstone, 1995

(20) 'Parents seek right to let their son die.' The Guardian 31 August 1991 and also Patrick Davies 'The Right to Die' British Journal of Nursing, vol 2 no 13 1993 (Pge 654)

(21) Graham Crow and Graham Allan 'Community Life - an introduction to local social relations' Harvester Wheatsheaf 1994 (Pge 167)

(22) Ibid. (Pge 169)

(23) J. Dale Munro 'Training Families in the "Step Approach Model" for effective advocacy' Canada's Mental Health, March 1991 (Pges 1-6)

(24) Glenda Fine and Joyce Borden 'Parents involved in network project: support and advocacy training for parents' chapter in Friedman, Duchnowski and Henderson (editors) 'Advocacy on behalf of children with serious emotional problems' Florida 1989 (pges 68-78)

(25) Robert and Martha Perske 'Hope for the Families - new directions for parents of persons with retardation or other disabilities' Abingdon 1973 (Pge 89)

(26) Sheila Jupp 'Working with Parents of Children with Severe Learning Difficulties' chapter three in John Harris (Editor) 'Innovations in Educating Children with Severe Learning Difficulties' Brothers of Charity, Lisieux Hall 1993

(27) Kenneth Thurman and Anne Widerstrom 'Infants and Young Children with Special Needs' Paul Brookes, 1990 (Pge 276)

(28) W. J. Hardeman 'A Family Council in a Psychiatric Hospital' unpublished paper Utrecht, October 1987

(29) Kenn Jupp 'Living a full Life with Learning Disabilities' Souvenir Press 1994 (Pge 151)

(30) Ibid. (Pge 157)

(31) Ibid. (Pge 161)

(32) Robert and Martha Perske Ibid. (Pge 23)

(33) Garry Hornby 'Counselling in Child Disability - skills for working with parents' Chapman & Hall (Pge 171 and also chapter 7 on assertion skills)

(34) 'The Local Government Ombudsman - annual report 1993-4' The Commission for Local Administration in England, 1994 (Pges 15-16)

(35) Robert and Martha Perske Ibid. (Pge 81)

(36) Alan Leighton (Editor) 'Mental Handicap in the Community' Woodhead Faulkner 1988 (Pges 46-7)

(37) Ann Richardson *et al.* 'A New Deal for Carers' Kings Fund 1989 (Pge 87)

(38) P.R. Roos 'Advocate Groups' in J.L. Matson and J.A. Mulick (Editors) 'Handbook of Mental Retardation' Pergamon Press, 1983 (Pges 23-35)

(39) RADAR Bulletin 'RNIB Advocacy Service for Parents' vol 219, September 1992, (pges 7-8)

(40) H. Rutherford Turnbull *et al.* 'Disability and the Family - a guide to decisions for Adulthood' Paul Brookes 1989 (Pges 293-312)

(41) 'Exploring Patient Advocacy' THS November 1992 (Pge 7)

(42) There are some exceptions to this, for example, see Tim and Wendy Booth 'Parenting under Pressure: Mothers and Fathers with Learning Difficulties' Open University Press 1994

(43) Laura Middleton 'Children First - working with children and disability' Venture Press 1992 (Pge 47)

(44) See for example Loring Brinckerhoff 'Self Advocacy: a critical skill for students with learning disabilities' Community Health (USA) 16(3) 1993 (Pges 23-33) which looks at the ways parents dominate decision making in schools and colleges and incidentally using the term 'learning disability' in an entirely different sense to this side of the pond.

(45) Joy McCallam 'The Forgotten People - carers in three minority ethnic communities in Southwark' Kings Fund 1990 (Pges 72-3)

(46) Daphne Wood 'MIND's Policy on Black and Minority Ethnic People and Mental Health' MIND 1993

(47) Marsha White 'When will the pain go away?' Community Living, July 1994 (Pges 20-23)

(48) J. Twigg 'Carers Research and Practice' HMSO 1992 and also by the same author 'Models of Carers' Journal of Social Policy, vol 18, Part 1, January 1989 (Pge 55)

(49) Norman Warner 'Community Care: just a fairy tale?' Carers National Association, 1994 (Pge 18)

FIVE: SELF ADVOCACY:

'We have a voice and must learn to use that voice and be listened to. We must help people take more control over their lives.'

Anya Sousa
'Young People First' 1993

Anya Sousa worked for the Downs Syndrome Association for several years. She has experienced at first hand the discrimination against people with learning difficulties. With her mothers help, she has struggled against prejudice all her life. About ten years ago she was knocked down by a motor bike. As they were putting the blanket over her in the street, the ambulance person said "Why are they letting this Downs Syndrome woman walk about on her own?"

Her mother, who died four years ago, fought a High Court action against her daughter's exclusion from mainstream education. The headmistress at one school commented "Why have I got to have this Mongol in my school?" She had bad experiences in a special school. The other children called her names and picked on her. She was told to stuff toy rabbits when she was capable of much more complex tasks. "The teachers told us what to do. They never listened to us or saw what our real abilities really were. In the mainstream school I passed three CSEs and went on to college to study office skills and also cooking and waitressing. Later I appeared on Channel Four television news to prove that people with Down's Syndrome could do office work. Now I live on my own in a flat in London with some help from my sisters. I can work and live independently. I can go on holiday if I like. No one can tell me what to do or how to live my life."

Anya now works full time for Young People First (YPF), a self advocacy organisation set up early in 1993 to cater for people between the ages of sixteen and thirty. Currently, it is mainly London based but hopes to become more national in the near future. Anya says: "We have a voice and must learn to use that voice and be listened to. We must help people take more control over their lives. We have to learn about our rights and what we have to do to look after ourselves and our things. We must help young people take more control of their lives. We aim to teach others who make decisions about us to listen to us." (1)

YPF has close links with People First and is currently helping to write a course on safe sex. It also runs courses for people in day centres and elsewhere. It supports a group working on assessments in a Greenwich school. It is collaborating with the Open University on a new course. It hopes to run conferences for people with Downs Syndrome. It has done some TV, magazine and newspaper work to publicise the achievements of people with a learning difficulty.

Self advocacy, as Anya practises it, is so simple to define and yet so complex. It is the oldest form of advocacy which each of us uses every-day unself-consciously - speaking out for ourselves; asserting our wishes to others. "I don't want that; I want this . . ." In another way, it is very difficult to define because it merges so invisibly into ordinary communication. It struggles both internally and externally against ablism. There is much to tackle. Murphy notes that the most-far-reaching changes in the consciousness of disabled people are: 'lowered self-esteem; the invasion and occupation of thought by physical deficits; a strong undercurrent of anger; and the acquisition of a new, total, and undesirable identity.' (2) All this contributes to a tendency to be passive; to accept injustice, to complain rarely and simply to put up with things.

But take this conventional definition: 'A social movement organized and controlled by mentally retarded people with the assistance of non-handicapped advisers who actively promote the efforts of mentally retarded people to achieve equality, independence, and recognition as full-fledged members of society; and work to ensure and protect legislated civil rights and basic rights of consumer participation by mentally retarded consumers of human services.' (3) This isn't an everyday activity. It reeks of group meetings which lobby powerful persons and bodies for better conditions. It describes a process more usually called 'collective' advocacy. One of the major confusions is that the term is commonly used in two quite distinct contexts - about the assertion of individuals and also about groups getting together to voice common concerns.
Dowson identifies four different themes:

1) Self-advocacy as a very specific and individual act. A person assumed to have no voice, or nothing to say, speaks; and so challenges the identity they have been assigned.

2) Self-advocacy as one component of some more general activity. Thus a case review or Individual Plan meeting might involve (and indeed should involve) self-advocacy as one part of a process which also includes information-sharing, decision making, and service allocation.

3) Self-advocacy as a group activity, in which the members represent themselves and their immediate peers; some users of an ATC, for example, who meet to discuss issues of special concern to those who attend the centre.

4) Self-advocacy as campaigning for people with learning difficulties as a whole. (4)

These various and different strands lead to considerable confusion with the boundaries of collective advocacy as we shall see more fully later. Anya is not only involved in uncovering her own individual power, in tackling personal oppression but also, through People First, in joining with others to campaign on more general issues.

The formal concept of self-advocacy has developed mainly in the fields of learning difficulties and mental health. However, the Greater London Association of Disabled People (GLAD) runs self-advocacy training primarily aimed at young physically disabled people. 'The courses cover language and images of disability, discrimination, rights and legislation, developing assertion and communication skills, groups and committees, and devising and implementing plans.' (5) It was discovered that 'many of the young disabled people interviewed had no notion of their rights, the need to be able to make decisions or any levels of disability awareness'. (6)

The objectives for self advocacy were seen as:

1. to learn how to become assertive and empowered so they are able to take control over their own lives.
2. to make their own representation to social services and the various service providers which they will have to confront for the rest of their lives
3. to ask for support in a way which does not compromise the control they have over their own lives. (7)

There are also some self advocacy schemes in the elderly services. 'Advocacy for older people is concerned with the empowerment of individual people . . . Older people are entitled to the help that they need to improve their sense of well-being and to retain control over their own lives. In most cases this may be in the form of information, occasional representation and the support of an individual's own self advocacy . . . self advocacy groups could be established in day centres, residential or hospital settings or structured around specialist advice/problem-solving sessions.' (8)

Perske writes movingly of a simple experience of plain soundless communication. 'From an Open Letter to Robert Williams: Eleven years ago, you and I sat together at a government hearing in Hartford, Connecticut. You had your board with the alphabet and words on it, and you began to spell sentences with your finger. Right then, you became more interesting to me than all the oral garbage that filled the air that day. You - with that educated finger - cut through the verbiage to the central issues and the real right or wrong of them. Next came meetings in Washington, DC, where I spied you on the fringe of the crowd, quietly waiting until all the "talkers" had left. Then, with your communication board between us, I learned to slow down, to watch, to listen, and to be enlightened and feel strangely relaxed.' (9) Much literature is preoccupied with the ways in which people with disabilities must adapt their communication patterns to be understood. Refreshingly, Perkse concentrates on the very considerable changes that able-bodied people have to make.

PEOPLE FIRST

The modern origins of the self advocacy movement lie in the social clubs established by people with learning difficulties in Sweden in the early 1960s. These were run by their members. Clubs organised regional meetings to share ideas and experiences and there followed two successful national conferences in 1968 and 1970. (10) People First, the international self advocacy movement, began in the United States. 'The origins of the self advocacy movement for people with mental retardation are principally found in 1973 at the Fairfield state institution for mentally retarded people in Salem, Oregon. A group of residents at this institution were preparing to live in the community and wanted to develop a support system with their peers. With the help and encouragement of some interested social workers, serving as advisers, the residents began learning basic organizing skills that culminated in the first convention run by and for people with mental retardation.' In just over ten years, there were over 5,000 persons active in self-advocacy groups in the United States and Canada, mainly under the umbrella name of People First. (11)

In June 1993, almost 1400 self-advocates and their supporters from thirty two countries met in Toronto, Canada at the third international conference of People First. John Jacobs from Los

Angeles summed up their demands: **integration** (in real homes in the community), **productivity** (in real jobs paying proper wages), and **inclusion** (in mainstream services and facilities). (12)

The movement had spread to Britain by the early 1970s through the participation forums and conferences organised by Mencap and CMH (Campaign for Mentally Handicapped People now called Values into Action). Nine self advocates from this country went to the first international conference in Takoma, Washington State, USA, in 1984 and London People First held its first meeting in the same year.(13) By 1980, some 22% of adult training centres had some form of self advocacy group; by 1986/7 this percentage had risen to over 60%. (14) Some early and robust battles were fought around the stigmatising term 'mental handicap', to which professionals were attached. They discovered that 'language can hurt' and that 'self definition can be empowering.' (15) Self-advocates succeeded gradually in having it replaced by the less negative terms 'learning difficulties' or 'learning disabilities'.

An important text about self advocacy developments in both the UK and USA detailed the great personal cost to self advocates: 'A theme that has come out of many self-advocacy meetings and conferences is that speaking up for oneself has costs. People are vulnerable and can be hurt, and often they need a lot of consistent, long-term support.'(16) Edgerton puts the root problem so concisely: 'No other stigma is as basic as mental retardation in the sense that a person so labelled is thought to be completely lacking in basic competence.'(17)

This rapidly expanding movement had several core ingredients. It fosters peer support through the regular group meetings. It has non-disabled advisers who help in the development of various organising skills. It has several characteristics, closer to self-help groups than what so far has been understood as advocacy:

* open and permissive communication with people who have experienced the same problem or condition and societal reactions to it

* enhanced opportunities for socialization of individuals who are otherwise frequently isolated and alienated

* social learning of coping abilities from peers who are successfully living with the condition

* reduction of the social distance traditionally maintained by professionals in a therapeutic relationship

* providing a forum for new members to emulate veteran peer role models, and veteran members to receive reinforcement from new members.(18)

Put more simply and more eloquently by the former President of London People First: 'Self advocacy enables us to make choices and make our decisions and control the way our lives should be made.' (19) This means learning essentially to be less passive and more assertive:

> 'the right to ask for what we want realising that others have the right to say no.
> the right to have an opinion, feeling and emotions and to express them appropriately.
> the right to make statements which have no logical basis and which we do not have to justify.
> the right to make our own decisions and to cope with the consequences.
> the right to choose whether or not to get involved in the problems of someone else.
> the right not to know about something and not to understand
> the right to make mistakes.
> the right to privacy.' (20)

In these various self advocacy groups, the role of the adviser is vital. Dowson and Whittaker outline some of the dilemmas: 'The adviser's ability to allow the group to decide when to engage in action can easily, and even unconsciously, be affected by other concerns. The adviser with righteous anger or missionary zeal may be impatient to get started. More often, the prospect of clashing with "the system" - especially with one's own colleagues - will be worrying, and it will be tempting to hold the group back.'

'The duty of the adviser to follow their role and respect the right of the group to make its own decisions, does not mean that the adviser is obliged to sit and do nothing while the group rushes headlong in the wrong direction. Part of the role is to offer information and advice, to set out the options and to suggest the advantages of each one. Inevitably this will often involve expressing a personal opinion, and sometimes it may be important to the adviser to declare their own feelings.' (21)

Self advocates describe the nature of a good group, outlining a healthy mix between task and process:-

'Everyone says something - everyone is involved
The group belongs to the members - the group is in charge, not the adviser
The adviser doesn't talk unless invited to do so
People share problems
The adviser is not there!
The meetings should be interesting - have action - make changes
The meetings should be fun!
The group does what the self-advocates want, not what the adviser says
People should take turns to speak - speak up clearly and not too fast
The group provides the right help for people who can't walk/speak/hear, e.g. Minutes on tape as well as written.' (22)

Initially the social experience of getting together, the emotional buzz may be sufficient. However, for most group members, there needs to be some action; an experience of trying to make changes both within individual situations as well as within the services. In Wrexham, a self advocacy group for all people with disabilities, recorded some practical achievements:

*   two people have started to meet people outside their homes for the first time in years
*   one person found out he was not receiving his full benefit entitlement
*   two others have followed up their eligibility for the Disabled Living Allowance
*   two more are pressing for housing adaptations
*   writing articles for the local newsletter on disability issues
*   produced a leaflet asking people not to park in disability parking bays
*   organising information stall at a local fair
*   visiting members who are in hospital. (23)

On a more collective and structural level, increasing numbers of self advocacy groups have been involved in discussions about the Care in the Community legislation with social services departments. Northamptonshire People First liaised with the Assistant Director and the Community Care Planning Officer between early December and mid-February 1993-4. The achievements were described as:

'Giving them a run for their money'; 'Members developed a broader understanding of community care and the consultation process'; and 'raised the profile of People First within the department'. (24)

SURVIVORS

These developments and confusions were echoed, to some extent, in the mental health movement. In the 1960s and 70s, there were a number of halting attempts through what were primarily collective advocacy organisations like the Mental Patients Union (MPU) and Cope. MPU's manifesto stated strongly: 'Many people are treated to make them shut up. Treatment can be a form of punishment.' 'We believe that patients should have the right to decide their own best interests and not have this taken away by the hospital bureaucracy . . . We think that the way hospitals are organised in very large units, their ideas about mental illness, their lack of staff and facilities, does make life in the hospital a battle between the patients and the staff.' (25) Some attempts at user power were linked with the anti-psychiatry movement; others tried to develop structural understandings of the origins of mental illness. (26)

Survivors Speak Out (SSO) was the first fully national network of mental health service recipients. It tries to turn the misery and powerlessness into positive energy for change. The experiences of users is paramount. SSO originated at a MIND conference in 1985, immediately following the International Mental Health Charter 2000 conference in Brighton. Now it has a network of individual members and affiliated local self-help groups across England, Wales and Northern Ireland. There are two classes of membership - full membership for survivors of mental health services and associate membership for all others. (27)

Peter Campbell of SSO: 'As far as I'm concerned, self-advocacy in practice is about collective action for change. A lot of what I've been involved in is groups of people working together to define their wants, raising their self-confidence and their belief in the validity of their wants and then acting to secure them. What has been transforming for me in the last five or six years has been to be part of a collective action. No longer standing in the Charge Nurse's office, an isolated patient asking for my rights . . . but working with friends, locally, nationally, internationally, to secure for ourselves what is necessary and rightful.' (28)

SSOs first conference in September 1987 at Edale, produced a Charter of Needs and Demands which asked 'that mental health service providers recognise and use people's first hand experience of emotional distress for the good of others . . . Self advocacy is about power - about people regaining power over their own lives. The psychiatric system in this country seems peculiarly designed to deny power to those who enter it (or are sent into it) for help. Such powerlessness is then reinforced by the practices and attitudes of the wider society into which the recipients of services eventually emerge. Through self advocacy, through taking positive action for ourselves, we challenge this process, both by working to change the psychiatric system and by challenging our devalued status in the eyes of the majority of society'. (29)

By 1992, there were 'over 100 groups scattered around England, Wales and Scotland which could come under the heading of self-advocacy or user groups'. (30)   1988 saw the setting up of MINDLINK within the national MIND organisation. Its aims were to ensure user consultation and representation throughout the whole organisation.

Campbell argued several years ago that these various groups fell into four categories:

* those closely associated with services
* those devoted to establishing patient's councils and advocacy schemes
* action groups operating in a range of ways to improve local service provision
* regional or campaigning groups acting on issues such as the misuse of tranquillisers. (31)

He feels that the situation is much more complex nowadays. (32)

The various groups used different strategies. Some saw political perspectives as being vital; others wanted to use alternative thera-pies; others tried to reform the existing services whilst others wanted nothing to do with them.

Helen Smith wrote: 'Some groups are advocating user-run ser-vices and feel their experience of the psychiatric system as being one of disempowerment and restriction of rights . . . Other user groups are asking for involvement in monitoring services, training workers and representation in planning; seeking to influence services at a local level, they are not concerned to be directly involved in managing services . . . Some user groups are asking for changes not directly related to deficiencies in the health system, such as higher benefits or better employment opportunities . . . Other groups still, are asking for better services provided by the

71

psychiatric system such as improved out-patient facilities; or see their role as supporting other users within the advocacy framework.' (33)

Most groups promote a mixture of co-operation whilst maintaining some distance from the established services. The Brixton Community Sanctuary offers individual help towards increased self advocacy in the form of a pack, written by mental health service users. This helps individuals to develop and construct a profile of themselves; to assess the services they use; to judge their needs; to develop opportunities for them to take control of their lives; to provide advice and information so they can construct their own support network and care plan. (34) They promote a mixture of helping people towards self advocacy; using the existing systems; and constructing user-run alternatives.

O'Hagan accurately criticises the British movement for the sin of reformism and over close contacts with professionals. 'It is common for groups of survivors to admit professionals to their membership as "allies". In some groups the professionals have taken over... I am against admitting any other people to survivor groups. If any coalition with other groups takes place, a clearly identified survivor group, should be involved. Individual survivors, without the backing of their own group are likely to be swallowed up by others.'' (35) Campbell feels that this regrettable tendency is on the decline. (36)

The MIND guide comments: 'Advocacy is first and foremost a way of redressing the balance of power... It was sharing the experience of emotional pain and the distress caused by the impersonal and at times inhumane treatment, which turned a lot of sadness into anger. It allowed the self-advocacy movement of users and ex-users of the mental health services to emerge and to act collectively for the right to influence service provision.' (37) Those are fine sentiments, if much too premature. It is far too early to make any overall assessment of the influence of self-advocacy on mental health services or vice versa.

OBSTACLES

One major problem is the further exclusion of a variety of marginalised people, including most longstay patients. (38) So far they have played only a minor role in the advocacy movement. The movement runs the danger of mirroring aspects of an inherently racist and sexist society. The feminist element is strong and rightly demands some separate psychiatric services where distressed women can feel more secure. Women psychiatric survivors and their allies set up a number of projects in the early 1980s.

There are some inherent conflicts between the feminist and survivor movements. 'Even though survivors and feminists can exist happily side by side, contradictions occurred in the women's movement when they were blended together. The loss of faith in professionalism and therapy are central to survivor ideology and only peripheral to feminist ideology. Feminist mental health workers cannot be relied on to give credibility to our differences in ideological orientation; some do not even recognise them. White women have begun to recognise their role in the white oppression of Black women. Professional feminists need to recognise their role in the oppression of survivors.' (39) That will be a very difficult process, for example some leading feminists make a reasonable living from therapy.

The whole movement remains woefully short of ethnic minority members.(40) Determined efforts must be made to include them. There is much evidence of the 'double oppression in psychiatry'. 'Misdiagnosis and a fear of having emotional experiences or learning difficulties misrepresented by professional assessment as mental illness is documented among members of black and minority communities . . . Reach out and contact black users.' (41) 'We already have Afro-Caribbean and Irish survivor groups, women's and mental health professionals survivor networks. We will see other survivor groups of people who are badly served by the mental health services, such as people with hearing difficulties and people physically challenged in other ways.' (42) The Asian communities also have particular needs.

The movement must reach out also to those with more multiple and profound difficulties. There is an immense danger of the 'dictatorship of the articulate'. This means having to watch and listen a lot; learning to use tapes and picture materials. (43) Other disability groups are prevented from full participation by the difficulties of physical access and a shortage of relevant technology to facilitate communication. 'Deaf people are unnecessarily isolated and disabled by the general lack of awareness and lack of funding to make disabled people a full part of the community, via access to new technological equipment such as mini-coms etc.' (44) 'Both in the USA and this country, there are considerable problems with insufficient interpreters for doctors appointments, court appearances . . . ' (45)

Relationships between the disability groups are not always harmonious. It is sometimes difficult for people with mental health problems to get accepted within the disability movement. They raise complex issues about the essential meaning of disability. One prominent disabled athlete, Tanni Grey, argued for the exclusion of learning disabled athletes from the Paralympic Games. (46) Roger Biggs of the UK Sports Association for People with a Learning Disability, responded: 'To say that alternative provision should be made is akin to saying there should be a separate Olympic Games for black athletes. The issue is one of promoting equality of opportunity for all disabled athletes, irrespective of whether their impairment is based on physical, sensory or learning difficulties.' (47)

As we saw in the previous chapter, there are also problems within the families. They may feel threatened by the new assertiveness of their disabled members. 'Opposition to self-advocacy from families is at least in part due to carers fears of being marginalised. To them, the enthusiasm of professionals for listening to users can seem like an excuse to ignore carers. Being a carer is often not an easy role. New ideas on service provision come and go, and yet for most carers the responsibilities and the complex, often painful feelings remain . . . Most families will not have the chance to hear the arguments in favour of self advocacy.' (48) 'With the growing awareness of the importance of self-advocacy for young people from all minority groups, how can parents be helped to understand the need to help children and young people to "speak for themselves" and begin to make choices and take part in informed decision-making from an earlier age? How can the separate advocacy needs of parents and young people be resolved?' (49)

Professional reactions to self-advocacy are very mixed. 'Some joined as advisers or allies. But other observers suspected plots. . . The tactics of displaying the performing disabled person at the professional court or funding the tame self-advocacy group should not be underestimated in the armoury of the establishment's resistance to true empowerment. Only those changes which do not threaten the white "able" male professional's control of health and social welfare will be readily accepted. "Dangerous" elements, on the other hand, will be sucked into the system in a token acceptance. By a variety of subtle deals they will be compromised and caught up. When rendered harmless, "advocacy", "equal opportunities" and other change agents will be paraded in mainstream provision as evidence of the powerholders' commitment to power-sharing.' (50)

And further: 'Users asked to be on planning committees often find the agendas are already set, and the issues that we are concerned about are rarely on them. Professionals usually don't want to deal with the fundamental questions users raise. This is bound to cause conflict and disillusionment with the process.' (51)

Simons comments wisely: 'Not surprisingly, many service providers have a distinctly service-centred view of self-advocacy. Their implicit assumption is that it is all about commenting on services; a sort of service development tool that needs to be organised in the most efficient way using structures that mimic and feed into their own decision-making systems. This is a perspective that sits uncomfortably with the concept of self-advocacy as a grass roots user movement.' (52) There are so many issues, perhaps the most important like employment and housing, which effect the ordinary lives of disabled people which have little directly to do with the conventional services.

As a unified movement, self-advocacy is a creative hotchpotch of different approaches struggling against inflexible services. 'First, the movement has the goal of inculcating into the collective consciousness of both the lay public and professional communities a recognition that people with mental retardation are, first and foremost, members of the human community who have both rights and responsibilities. Second, the movement has the goal of helping mentally retarded people obtain opportunities for employment and other adult-life activities comparable to those of people who are not disabled. Third, the movement has the goal of integrating retarded individuals into the mainstream of American life. And finally, the movement seeks to overcome the image of people with a mental retardation as being members of a devalued population.' (53)

Self-advocacy can be an effective way of challenging the existing stereotypes. Both the media and professionals tend to depict them as victims rather than people with power. Rogers and Pilgrim complain that social policy commentators ignore the potentiality of empowerment movements. 'Instead, usually a picture is painted of passive, vulnerable consumers, who are being increasingly denied the benevolent care of hospital-based professionals.' (54) That conflicts fundamentally with bold photos of a leather-jacketed man in a wheelchair with a 'Crip with a Chip' placard.

Historically the victim perception was always a very partial truth. For example, 'Betsy Bell was admitted to Brockhall mental handicap hospital, near Blackburn in October 1959 because "she was difficult to manage". She sang me some protest songs. "One ward sister was cruel. As punishment, she put a female patient in a cold water bath. The poor patient died later. She used to put girls in side rooms. Once I got into trouble. I walked off down the road.

Somebody had upset me. One of the nurses brought me back. They put me in the side room. I was locked in with just a bed. I was frightened. They brought me regular meals and let me out after a few days. I learnt my lesson and never ran off again."

"The staff punished you in other ways. We got a weekly payment of £2.50 for working on the ward. We washed tables and set them. One nurse made me carry plates and cups and meals on my walking frame. She used to boss us about. I dropped them often. I wasn't so steady. You had to make yourself useful. If you cheeked staff, they took the weekly money away or put you on strong medicine. They used to give you largactil syrup. They gave it to quieten and calm you down. It was a nasty sweet taste. You got it for shouting and arguing. It made you go to sleep - dopey.

'Did you ever hear of the old songs we used to sing in Brockhall Hospital?

> Come to Brockhall
> come to Brockhall
> It's a place of misery
> Round the corner there's a signpost
> saying welcome home to me.
> Don't believe it
> don't believe it
> It's a pack of dirty lies
> If it weren't for Dr **
> we would be in Paradise.
> Build a bonfire
> build a bonfire
> put the Matron on the top
> put the staff in the middle
> and to burn the bloody lot.'''

(Sung to the tune of Clementine).(55)

ISSUES

Self-advocacy is the central process which the other forms work towards; helping oppressed people to speak for themselves so that they can gain power. There are some continual conflicts with advocacy by families and that by service professionals. Each one may have hidden agendas of their own. Will they be willing to give up the vicarious power they possess ? I have often been in rooms with the parents of teenage sons and daughters with learning difficulties. It has been very hard to hear their children express anything because the parents were on automatic advocacy pilot. "He thinks this. He feels that . . ." sometimes drowns out the person directly concerned to express his or her own views.

There may also be substantial conflicts with professional advocates. O'Hagan notes: 'In New Zealand we did advocacy for people in hospital and the survivor who did it ran around with far too much work to do. People became very dependent on him. I saw we were just perpetuating the same old thing . . . If you are an advocate with an office and a big diary in your hand, survivors think you have special powers to help; they are immediately disempowered and become dependent - even if you are a survivor. But if instead, we had done workshops with a support group on assertiveness or ways to support each other or the Mental Health Act, we would just be facilitating a process where people could discover and use their own competence. Giving survivors skills and information, rather than just using yours on their behalf, means they can take more control over their lives.' (56)

It may be very difficult to develop self- advocacy with groups like those having Alzheimer's Syndrome; those with severe head injuries and with profound disabilities. We shall never ever know whether Tony Blair , injured at the Hillsborough football ground, would have wanted to die. In another century, it may be possible to revive him from the coma to an active life. Even so we have to pay continuous and sensitive attention to what the wishes of those who cannot speak for themselves might be, rather than take the easy pathway - what we consider to be the best. With someone who has no or very little speech, their wishes and preferences can be constantly expressed, just spitting out cornflakes at the breakfast table is an expression of choice.

Some groups and individuals may not even see themselves as disabled. Some people receiving treatment for a 'mental illness' may see the sickness in society rather than inside their minds. 'Many deaf project participants said that some deaf people do not define themselves as "disabled" and might feel that consultation exercises by "disability" related planning teams did not apply to them.' (57)

Self-advocacy can be tokenistic. People attend groups which achieve nothing and never really had any chance of real influence. The groups are held on service premises, run by service staff with no possibility of power. What use is self-advocacy if nothing changes? Oppressed people get dispirited if no one listens or responds. Talking and expressing feelings are just a beginning. Most want action. Managers need to work towards more-responsive services which react sensitively and speedily. Service users can be involved at all levels of decisions; service planning, project management, as well as at the individual review meetings, if they are to have genuine power and influence.

There are often fundamental disagreements between some radical users, relatives and professionals. How can there be partnership between groups which hold such contrasting views and radically different degrees of power and influence? For example how would you square this view of mental illness with the dominant medical model? 'We should explore a total other direction. My fancy is that it could be a cultural movement where we defend the right to be mad and give some positive attribution to it instead of nurturing the idea that somebody should actually get well again. People have the right to be who they are; they have the right to be mad. If being mad is put on the same level as being Black or being homosexual or being a woman, I think that would be a far better approach; to bring madness out of the back rooms and into the open. Therefore you have to create a culture of mad people.' (58)

Difficulties may also arise for advisers and allies. 'Is it ethical to raise learners' expectations when these may not be able to be met because of lack of resources or well-planned provision, or hostility from other service-providers? Conflicts within organisations or between different professionals can arise over risk-taking or the sharing of confidential information... In what ways is it possible for professionals to demystify their specialist knowledge and skills and make them available to learners on a more egalitarian basis?'(59) 'Self-advocacy demands much from professionals. It is inherently fragile, usually patchily and inconsistently funded and services watch it like a vulture watches an injured antelope. It depends on a very few vulnerable people who pay large costs for its survival.' (60)

References
(1) Personal interview with Anya Sousa and an article by Anya in 'Our Lives, Our Decisions' Care Weekly, 2 September 1993
(2) R.F. Murphy 'The Body Silent' Holt 1987 (Pge 108)
(3) C. Rhoades 'Self Advocacy: Readings on Self Advocacy groups of people with developmental disabilities' University of Oregon Rehabilitation Research and Training Centre on Mental Retardation 1985 (Pges 19-20)
(4) Steve Dowson 'Keeping it Safe: self advocacy by people with learning difficulties and the response of services' Values into Action 1991
(5) Personal communication from Gary Parr, Advocacy Co-ordinator, GLAD, 14 January 1994

(6) GLAD 'Speaking for Ourselves' 1990 (Pge 9)

(7) Jacqui Christy 'Speaking for Ourselves' GLAD 1993

(8) Age Concern 'Speaking up for Yourself! Putting advocacy into Practice' 1991

(9) Robert Perske 'Circles of Friends - people with disabilities and their friends enrich the lives of one another' Abingdon 1988

(10) H. Rutherford Turnbull *et al* .'Disability and the Family - a guide to decisions for Adulthood' Paul Brookes 1989 (Pge 315)

(11) Richard Wood 'Speaking up for yourself - putting advocacy into practice' Age Concern 1991

(12) Wendy and Tim Booth 'People First celebrate their success stories' Community Living, October 1993 (Pges 14-15)

(13) Andrea Whittaker, Janet Wright and Gary Bourlet 'Setting Up for Self-Advocacy' chapter six in Tim Booth (editor) 'Better Lives - changing services for people with learning difficulties' Social Services Monographs, 1990 (Pge 79)

(14) Quoted in Bronach Crawley 'Self Advocacy Manual - an overview of the development of self-advocacy by Mentally Handicapped People and recommendations for the development of Trainee committees' Hester Adrian 1982 and Bronach Crawley 'The Growing Voice: a survey of self advocacy - groups in adult training centres and hospitals in Great Britain' CMH publications 1988

(15) Jennie Sutcliffe and Ken Simons 'Self Advocacy and Adults with Learning Disability' National Institute of Adult Continuing Education, 1993

(16) Paul Williams and Bonnie Shoultz 'We can speak for Ourselves' Souvenir Press 1982 and 1991 (Pge 252)

(17) Robert Edgerton 'The Cloak of Competence' University of California Press 1973 (Pge 201)

(18) M.E. Jacques and K.M. Patterson 'The self help group model: a review' Rehabilitation Counselling Bulletin, 18, 1974 (pp 48-58)

(19) Gary Bourlet in Ken Simons 'Sticking up for yourself - self advocacy and people with learning difficulties' Community Care/Rowntree, November 1992

(20) From Lancashire Advocacy Development and Support Service: 'Speak Out for Yourself - report of a self advocacy conference in Lancashire' March 1993

(21) Steve Dowson and Andrea Whittaker 'On One Side - the role of the adviser in supporting people with learning difficulties in self-advocacy groups.' Values into Action in association with the King's Fund Centre, 1993 (Pges 13-16)

(22) Ibid. (Pge 9)

(23) WRAP 'Developing community based self advocacy Groups: first report' Speak Up Now, Wrexham Advocacy Partnerships, July 1991

(24) Kings Fund Centre: Community Care Group 'Information Exchange on Self Advocacy and User Participation' No 5, May 1993 (Pge 21)

(25) Mental Patients Union: 'Your Rights in Mental Hospital' Manchester Mental Patients Union, published in the early 1970s

(26) See for example Jan Wallcraft 'Origins of the Psychiatric Patients' Movement' in 'Training and user involvement in mental health services' NHS training directorate, 1992 (Pge 5) as well as the People not Psychiatry movement initiated in July 1969, see Michael Barnett 'People Not Psychiatry' Allen & Unwin 1973

(27) Mike George 'Do it Yourself' Community Care, 9 May 1991

(28) Peter Campbell 'Self Advocacy - working together for change' Presentation to MIND annual conference, 1990

(29) 'Self Advocacy Pack: empowering mental health service users' Survivors Speak Out, 1988

(30) Jan Wallcraft Ibid. 1992 (Pge 6-7)

(31) Peter Campbell 'Mental Health Self Advocacy in the United Kingdom' a chapter in V. Franson (editor) 'Mental Health Services in the United States and England: struggling for change' 1991 (Pges 155-161)

(32) Peter Campbell Personal Communication 11 September 1994

(33) Helen Smith 'Collaboration for Change' Kings Fund, January 1988

(34) Brixton Community Sanctuary 'Direct Power' 1994

(35) Mary O'Hagan 'Stopovers - on my way home from Mars' Survivors Speak Out, 1993 (Pge 73)

(36) Ibid. Peter Campbell Personal Communication

(37) 'The MIND Guide to Advocacy in Mental Health' MIND 1992

(38) See for example Althea and David Brandon 'Consumers as Colleagues' MIND 1987

(39) Mary O'Hagan Ibid. 1993 (Pge 37)

(40) Chris Harrison 'Black People and Self Advocacy' New Directions, Summer 1991

(41) Geraldine Hucka and Tom McAusland 'Issues for Women, Black and Minority Groups' in 'Training and User Involvement in Mental Health Services' 1993

(42) Viv Lindow 'Participation and Power' Open MIND, no 44 April/May 1990

(43) Kings Fund 'Information Exchange on Self-Advocacy and User participation - services to people with learning difficulties' November 1993

(44) Bob Peckford 'Workshop on Advocacy in the Deaf Community' in "Speaking out for Advocacy: a report of the National Conference' Labyrinth 1994

(45) Larry Orloff USA Personal communication August 1994

(46) Tanni Grey 'Professional Eye, Sport', The Observer 17 July, 1994

(47) Roger Biggs letter in The Observer 31 July, 1994 (Pge 20)

(48) Ken Simons 'Sticking up for Yourself - self advocacy and people with learning difficulties' Rowntree Foundation 1992 (Pge 74)

(49) Pat Hood 'Self Advocacy and Advocacy for parents of young people with disabilities and special needs' Further Education Unit 1989

(50) Julie Gosling 'Speaking Out' Nursing Times 12 February, vol. 88, no 7, 1992 (Pges 63-4)

(51) Jan Wallcraft Ibid. (Pges 8-9); also on this theme Andrea Whittaker 'Involving People with Learning Difficulties in Meetings' in L. Winn (Editor) 'Power to the People" Kings Fund 1990 (Pges 41-48)

(52) Ken Simons Ibid. (Pge 71)

(53) Craig Fiedler and Richard Antonak: chapter 2 in J.L. Matson and J.A. Mulick (Editors) 'Handbook of Mental Retardation' Pergamon Press, New York, 1986 (Pges 23-32)

(54) Anne Rogers and David Pilgrim 'Mental Health and Citizenship' in 'Improving Mental Health Practice' CCETSW 1993 (Pge 97)

(55) David Brandon 'Strange Places' University College Salford 1991 (Pges 16-19)

(56) Mary O'Hagan Ibid. 1993 (Pge 82)

(57) Catherine Bewley and Caroline Glendinning 'Involving disabled people in community care planning' Joseph Rowntree Foundation 1994 (Pge 27)

(58) quoted in Mary O'Hagan Ibid. 1993 (Pge 19)

(59) Further Education Unit 'Self Advocacy Skills for People with Disabilities' FEU June 1989

(60) H. Rutherford Turnbull Ibid. (Pges 321-2)

SIX: CITIZEN ADVOCACY

"A citizen advocate is a valued citizen who is unpaid and independent of human services creates a relationship with a person who is at risk of social exclusion and chooses one or several of many ways to understand, respond to, and represent that person's interests as if they were the advocate's own thus bringing their partner's gifts and concerns into the circles of ordinary human life.'

John O'Brien 'Learning from Citizen Advocacy Programs'
Georgia Advocacy Office, Georgia, USA, 1981

ORIGINS

The general concept of advocacy by a concerned citizen volunteer originated in Scandinavia in the 1950s.(1) But the specific technical concept arose in 1966 at a national conference for parents for children with cerebral palsy in Pennsylvania, USA. They asked the vital question 'What will happen to my child when I'm gone?' It seemed desirable that when there was no family, willing or able to protect a disabled person's interests, they should be protected in some other way. Wolf Wolfensberger, who attended this conference, suggested the rudiments of citizen advocacy - 'an unpaid citizen who had no connection with the service provided to that person, thus avoiding any conflict of interest.' (2) Interestingly, this suggestion was rejected by the conference. (3)

The first citizen advocacy (CA) program was established by the Capitol Association for Retarded Children in Lincoln, Nebraska, in 1970. In the following year, Wolfensberger had worked out details for the general structure and development. This involved 'a volunteer representing the interests of another person who had difficulty in meeting either his or her instrumental or expressive needs'. The advocate formed a one to one relationship with the person in need, termed a 'protégé'. (4)

Wolfensberger defined six desirable characteristics for advocates:

---

* a history of community residential stability
* a willingness to participate in a programme orientation
* an understanding of the specific advocacy role
* commitment to the advocacy mission
* a good moral character (5)

These characteristics, along with others, became the criteria for the recruitment of suitable volunteers by the National Association for Retarded Citizens. (6) It spread fairly rapidly in the United States, especially in the southern states like Georgia where it echoed the civil rights movement. The oppression of many disabled people seemed analogous to that of black people. By 1977 there were 142 local CA offices in 32 states involving 5,000 matches between advocates and protégés. There were also projects in both Canada and Australia, based on principles detailed by the two main pioneers - Wolf Wolfensberger and John O'Brien. (7)

In June 1981, the UK Advocacy Alliance, later to become National Citizen Advocacy, was launched consisting of five major voluntary agencies - MIND, MENCAP, One to One, the Spastics Society and the Leonard Cheshire Foundation. (8) This immediately followed the major TV documentary 'Silent Minority' exposing terrible conditions in two large mental handicap hospitals - St Lawrence's, near London and Borocourt, near Reading. (9) The Alliance pioneered citizen advocacy in three hospitals in the London area, which by 1983 included St Lawrence's. (10) A similar scheme, also for people with learning difficulties, began in Sheffield in 1984, which used advocates in the community as well. (11)

AIMS AND METHODS

Citizen advocacy aimed to empower socially excluded people by linking them with a volunteer, who was a 'valued person'. O'Brien defined a 'valued person' as someone 'richly connected to the networks of people and associations that make up community life and willing and able to act with - and perhaps for - another person. CA experience shows that people are rich in these valuable capacities regardless of social class, race, sex, and level of formal education'. (12) The debate about the meaning of 'valued' has echoed down the years. It is often used, less so latterly, to exclude a long list of the members of so called devalued groups including homosexuals, former prisoners and psychiatric patients.

CA is rooted in each local community through a Board formed of people unconnected with health, social services and voluntary organisations, which the potential protégés might use. Advocates must be entirely free to press the cases of individuals without impediment. The Board must educate themselves and their community in CA and eventually gain funding for an office run by a co-ordinator who has contact with people needing advocacy and makes 'matches' with relevant 'valued persons'.

In Britain, many CA groups were usually developed by professionals, particularly in the field of learning difficulties, who did have such vested interests. One early Board was chaired by a professional psychologist who didn't even live locally. Often, these people had few local contacts, lived out of town and so the schemes might have poor local roots. This was certainly the case with two projects with which we were connected in Greater Manchester and West Yorkshire.

The purpose of matches was to develop a close relationship between two individuals so that the rights and interests of the less powerful person could be defended and represented by the more powerful. 'Members of devalued groups are put in touch, on a one-to-one basis, with ordinary people who have their own place in the community, and who will listen to their point of view, respect their wishes, and stand with them to defend their rights. Individuals who have been stigmatised, ignored and made victims by society are thus enabled to assert themselves and become active members of their communities.'(13) These were brave and, as it turned out, overly ambitious aims.

People needing this support were located first. An advocate was then recruited exclusively for that individual and the CA co-ordinator arranged an initial meeting. Some took place in pubs or cafés; others in the advocate's or the co-ordinator's home. 'One immediate danger in matching, is to place too much pressure on both advocate and partner. Giving people space to determine their future involvement is of utmost importance. A long-term match will not evolve if pressure is used. It is a good idea to give the advocate and partner time to think it over, and then check with them their impression as to whether the relationship has potential . . . When both people have had the opportunity to chew things over and signal "yes, this is on", and their feelings correspond with those of the co-ordinator, it is a good idea to use a match letter. This clarifies the initial focus of the relationship and is an ideal opportunity to restate where the advocate's loyalty lies: that is to their partner, and not to the services they receive, service workers, or the citizen advocacy office.' (14)

The main task of the advocacy co-ordinator is to support these matches in unobtrusive ways, especially in the first few weeks and months. This is done through training and meetings with the advocate(s) but the co-ordinator must also have some direct channel through to the person with disabilities. If the match is not working properly, especially where there may be a question of exploitation, he or she must have a means of changing the situation and/or the advocate whilst avoiding the worst excesses of service evaluation and monitoring.

Funding organisations put considerable pressure on embryonic schemes. They want value for money, which usually means some measure of control. Frequently money is offered with strings attached. Among the most common strings are accountability to some form of service management; service agreements with the various professionals; information provided by advocates about their partners at meetings. All these conditions are unacceptable to Citizen Advocacy. (15)

The most colourful way of disseminating the CA essence is through stories. To give one relevant example: 'In February 1991, John had a domestic accident and spent two weeks in his local hospital burns unit, where he made a good recovery. While he was there, however, the consultant from the long-stay hospital where John used to live decided he should return to the hospital rather than his home in the community. An ambulance was booked to move him back to the hospital, although John thought he was going home.

Fortunately for John, he was represented by a married couple acting as joint advocates. They insisted that John be treated like any other person discharged from the burns unit and allowed to return to his home. The ambulance was cancelled and the advocates drove him home the next day, where he received the usual regular visits from the district nurse. At the same time the local newspaper phoned them to say they were planning a story under the headline "Mentally Handicapped Man sets fire to himself in Community Home". The advocates vehemently denied this claim and pointed out to the journalist that the newspaper was being used as a weapon in a political argument around the decision of where John should live. The journalist showed great interest in their advocacy role and agreed not to print the story.' (16)

The advocate should develop a feeling for the partner as an ordinary human being rather than as a damaged client or patient. The various service professionals are pressured into rather fragmented views of Ellen, Bob or Mary. They can see their various customers simply as a set of problems to be solved. He or she becomes yet another client or patient on a very long list. The advocate should get '. . . a sense of the person's undeveloped potential. She may decide that the person could communicate better, be more mobile, learn more functional skills, be more productive, or relate to a greater number of ordinary settings and ordinary people . . .

The citizen advocate believes that what others accept as part of a person's situation is unacceptable. He may conclude that there is nothing inherent in a person's handicap that justifies poor food, insufficient choices of clothing, overcrowded living quarters, work without pay, denial of necessary services, inactivity, or being moved from place to place without being consulted'. (17)

In Britain, CA is usually a long term partnership between an individual who has a disability and another who has not. It is a relationship between two people in which one person's loyalty is to one individual rather than to any service or organisation. CA schemes support citizen advocates as unpaid, independent volunteers, each representing only one individual. It is considered crucial that advocates should be not only independent of relevant services but also of the advocacy office, to minimise any potential clash of interest. This is a difficult balance. To ensure this precious independence and prevent CA becoming yet another sort of service, advocates should be:-

* 'supported by, but independent of, the local advocacy office and co-ordinator. For example, an obligation to submit regular reports may encourage advocates to feel that they are working for the office staff rather than for their partners'. The dynamic tension is that those same reports may be needed to justify further funding of the advocacy office.

* 'independent of the agencies and settings which provide services for their partners. Whenever there is a paid service, conflict of interest is inherent and would, for example, certainly arise if the advocate was paid to provide nursing care to their partner or to clean their room.' They would then be direct service providers.

* 'independent of the families of their partners in those instances where family interests are different. In this situation, it is vital for the partner to have an advocate who can strengthen their arguments and encourage the family to see their point of view. Close ties with any members of the family might inhibit an advocate'. (18) There are often perfectly natural tensions between families and their disabled member. The advocate always represents the disabled individual not the family but is **not** insensitive to their needs and the various emotional and practical links.

In view of this clear desire and real need for separation and independence, it is very curious that Wolfensberger once argued for advocates to be on the boards of human services. 'An effective strategy which helps ensure high-quality service provision is to have members of Citizen Advocacy, especially those who have protégés receiving an agency's services, sit on that agency's board of directors.'(19) It is not hard to see the considerable conflicts of vested interest which might arise from that ! It would lead inexorably into collective advocacy.

These general principles and structures of CA could be applied to those seen as powerless and oppressed but were mainly linked with the 'mentally retarded'. Their rights were frequently abused. Many were shut away in huge and isolated institutions, often excluded from education, work and leisure opportunities, denied basic human rights and stigmatised.

National Citizen Advocacy (NCA), recently renamed Citizen Advocacy Information and Training (CAIT), was formed from the original Advocacy Alliance in 1987. CAIT now concentrates on London and the South East. Other parts of the country are or will be covered by various regional groups. For example, SCOVO based in Cardiff covers Wales. There are currently 151 citizen advocacy schemes on the UK. database; nearly a third - 47 - are principally concerned with people with learning difficulties. More recently, there has been a growth of schemes working exclusively with those in mental distress - 29; 12 schemes work exclusively with those who are elderly; 4 with people who have a physical disability or sensory impairment. The remaining 59 work with more than one client group. (20)

Discussions began in the late 1980s, to develop a specific code of practice for elderly people. 'The emphasis will be on the needs of the consumer. Guidelines will be directed toward clarification of the relationship (both personal and legal) of the older person and their advocate and setting national standards for good practice.' (21) 'Age Concern has suggested that older people may be disempowered "by virtue of disability, frailty, marginalisation, institutionalisation, financial circumstances or even social attitudes".' (22) A small number of advocacy schemes are run by either Age Concern or the Alzheimers Disease Society. Often they are not fully independent schemes but modelled on CA principles. (23) 'Advocacy for older people in the UK. is still in its infancy but the infant is thriving and growing steadily.' (24)

One scheme began in the Stoke- on-Trent area in June 1989, and is now wholly funded by the Beth Johnson Foundation. There are eighteen partnerships supported by a co-ordinator. (25) Attempts to offer independent advocacy to mentally frail older people face broadly the sort of challenges experienced by advocates working with people with severe learning difficulties. Can an advocate represent the interests of someone apparently unable to communicate their needs and preferences in any comprehensible way or is unable to do so consistently ? We saw in an earlier chapter that Dworkin argued for the principle of substitute judgement. This means attempting to base decisions on the known values and beliefs of the dependent person when he/she had been still competent.

Since 1988, Camden Age Concern has assisted 'older people to articulate, defend or exercise their rights as citizens by linking them with specially selected and trained volunteers . . . Social attitudes towards older people tend to reinforce the assumption that as one grows older certain rights diminish or are lost. As we live and grow old among these attitudes this erosion of individual rights and self-esteem is often unopposed by the older person'. (26) This erosion occurs at the same moment when rights need to be clearer and stronger.

Staff can be hostile to advocacy. Their own emphasis may be on creature comfort and caring, not on maintaining any effective autonomy. Encouraging residents in an old people's home to make their own decisions can be very time consuming and troublesome. Some staff may see the various homes in which they work as their personal territory. 'There's a lot of "blaming the victim"; if people directly, or through an advocate, complain, or are seen as not fitting in to the way things are done, they can be seen as a problem. This can extend to being labelled as "mentally ill".' (27)

Camden has established fifteen formal CA matches. There are a number of more informal volunteers, often visiting more than one resident, based on particular old people's homes. Of the fifty residents at Ingestre Road elderly person home, about a dozen residents receive visits from five volunteers who see their role mainly as befriending. They were involved in helping residents choose another home as this one was closing temporarily for refurbishment. (28)

Projects for those with some physical disabilities are also developing. Peckford comments: 'English is a poor second language for many deaf people so little information in written form is accessible. Organisations like the British Deaf Association owned by disabled people attract less funding than "traditional" charities. Ideas take longer to get into the Deaf Community and it takes longer to find resources to put ideas into practice.' (29)

A three year advocacy project found that 'recruiting deaf advocates in a single locality is difficult because of the scattered nature of the Deaf Community . . . Many deaf people are coping with their own oppression and inequality . . . Many potential deaf advocates are themselves lacking in awareness of the channels by which they can redress grievances . . . meet barriers of non-accessible information. . . lack of understanding of the purpose of citizen advocacy . . . confused with befriending and social work'.(30) The Sense Advocacy project is a pilot scheme financed by Opportunities for Volunteering and the Kings Fund, which matches volunteer advocates with deaf-blind people who may also have a learning difficulty. It is based in the Horizon NHS Trust hospitals for people with a learning difficulty in St Albans and Radlett. (31)

There is a strong trend towards schemes which take people regardless of their perceived client group and use a variety of different methods. The Camberwell advocacy office was set up eight years ago as a straight CA project. It gradually diversified in order to survive and spread from forty or so active CA partnerships to a more diverse approach - involving direct advocacy; linked with care management; children's and young people's advocacy and self-advocacy. (32) The Kingston Advocacy Group is primarily concerned with mental health service users. It was initially formed as a purely CA organisation five years ago but diversified in to self-advocacy and professional advocacy. (33)

These multi-component and client group schemes need considerable resources and a good knowledge base which recognises the different issues in physical disability, mental health and learning difficulties . . . Sally Carr of CAIT sees 'the issues in mental health as more time limited; more urgent and related to crisis advocacy. They may need advocates with particular experience in that area. In Bromley, the majority of citizen advocates use or are still using mental health services. Those advocates may need understudies over a long period of time perhaps because of the tendency to need further help and support themselves . . . Many people wanting advocates are in crisis and seek urgent help through the CA co-ordinator . . . The advice of course is to have a ready pool of crisis advocates who can be deployed immediately, but this doesn't seem easy to achieve'. (34)

Many CA groups would like to develop a small pool of crisis advocates, available at short notice. They could offer support in emergency situations over a relatively short period of time, targeting events like homelessness, sudden sickness or discharge from or admission to any sort of institution. Advocates might have a particular knowledge or expertise in mental health or the legal structures. They are usually hard to recruit. (35) Llais in Wales describes short term work with a man with a learning disability and psychiatric problems who had been in and out of institutions most of his life. This man was afraid of a member of staff and also of being moved again. (36)

PURITY

Almost inevitably, as with any Wolfensberger innovation, questions arose early about purity. (37) It was seen that CA needed protection against those, especially from within the services, intent on adulteration, control and corruption. The main threat was to reduce or eliminate the sturdy advocacy component and turn it into a befriending scheme. However, this protection could use up vast amounts of energy. Sometimes it defends the letter rather than the spirit of CA, stifling any sort of innovation or departure from the original principles. Sometimes discussion echoed arguments over the Book of Genesis.

The citizen advocacy bible - Citizen Advocacy Program Evaluation (CAPE) laid down at considerable length what a citizen advocacy scheme was and also, for some people more importantly, what it was not. CAPE was intended as a comprehensive yardstick for monitoring and evaluating schemes. The manual outlined in great detail the five main principles of:

*   advocate independence;
*   program independence;
*   clarity of staff function;
*   balanced orientation to protégé needs;
*   positive interpretations of people who are handicapped.
(38)

In an odd way, it did not look much at what happens in the advocacy process. 'CAPE has its critics. It concentrates on the organisation, rather than on the advocates (though the latter are involved in CAPE exercises), which has left some commentators complaining that we know too little about the nature of the advocate/partner relationship.' (39) This seems a curious and central mystery about which the outsider (and probable non-believer) is not permitted to learn.

Increasingly this was linked with the rapidly developing body of literature on the normalisation principle on which Wolfensberger and O'Brien were also working. Their Program Analysis of Service Systems (PASS) was much concerned with purity. (40)

Such manuals proliferated rapidly. The Texas research institute on mental retardation devised three handbooks on how to set up an advocacy program; how to train volunteers and provide advocacy resources. (41)

O'Brien added his own 'Learning from Citizen Advocacy Programs' as a successor or supplement to CAPE. (42) This is a much more human document but still bulky. Rather ironically, apart from the last scrapbook section, it says little about the wide variety of things people in citizen advocacy relationships might actually achieve together. Only in the precious stories is there much sense of what goes on. No other part of the whole advocacy movement has so little to say about the process, and spends so much energy on excluding possible invaders and adulterators.

An early paper in Britain by Carle argued that 'Citizen advocacy is NOT group advocacy. Individuals and organisations often advocate on group issues like legislation, disability rights, employment. But citizen advocacy is a match between two people, in which the advocate's loyalty is to one specific individual'.(43) A typical plea for purity and close contact between co-ordinators and others, rather like making a circle with covered wagons in the Wild West: 'Because Citizen Advocacy is so vulnerable to perversions and misinterpretations such isolation is very dangerous. My own experience leads me to believe that if it were not for my connection with others in the citizen advocacy movement over the past eight years, I would probably be off on my own doing some very strange misinterpreted version of Citizen Advocacy . . .' (44) This plea has a curious evangelical religious flavour and fervour.

Molloy comments protectively: 'I hear that some who are promoting, establishing, and practising Citizen Advocacy appear to be deciding that it's all right to employ only the principles which suit what they want to do. For example: some are paying expenses to advocates; some have decided to exclude certain degrees of disability; some suggest that Citizen Advocacy should undertake an issue-related campaigning role.' He suggests that these are not necessarily wrong, 'they each have dangers and that organisations doing them should not use the term citizen advocacy'. (45) He added later: 'The first principle for any group contemplating Citizen Advocacy remains that they should only proceed if they can accept and develop the principles. If they cannot they should do whatever they think needs doing and call it something else.' (46) Don't change anything is a recipe for stagnation.

Sometimes this rigid implementation of principles leads to some difficult decisions. 'A lot of people cared about Peter, and they'd been delighted to see enormous improvements in his life, encouraged by a very good support service. But now they could see that the service was changing for the worse - so much worse that Peter's way of life was being threatened. He needed someone to help him defend his rights and wishes, and the best person was Pauline, who used to work with him, and so knew him very well. She went to the local CA scheme and asked to be accepted as an advocate for Peter. They checked with Social Services, who told them that Pauline still had official links with the Department, because she had an official arrangement to live with, and support, one of their clients. This was actually untrue: she shared the house informally and gave support as a friend. But the CA scheme accepted the information from the Department and refused to accept Pauline as an advocate. Pauline concluded that she couldn't act as an advocate.' (47)

Here we see worryingly that the local social services department is accepted as a final authority on decisions about who should or should not be an advocate, not only by the CA scheme but also by the advocate herself. It is not clear at all that there was any genuine clash of interest in this case. CA schemes are hardly protected from these extremely infectious service values by independent funding (hard to get anyway). This infection is like pollen in the summer air.

One example of what Molloy would certainly see as perceived adulteration comes from Canada. This moved citizen advocacy a considerable step towards collective advocacy. 'Group advocacy is the collective action of individual advocates, each with his/her own protégé. Such action is taken to secure improved service for their protégés, who have either the same need, or different needs, such as loneliness, special diets, etc., but who all live in the same facility. This type of advocacy is relatively uncommon. One example is that of a group of advocates who wanted a better service for their protégés in an institution. This group of advocates was advised to write letters, call, and ask for the services that they wanted. These actions had results that improved the institution in many ways.' (48) Here the citizen advocates are inspirationally working together to press for structural changes in a service.

Wheeler outlines some more general dangers. Negative outcomes emerge from:-

* **Paralysis of analysis**; co-ordinators are so afraid of not doing it the right way they don't do anything

* **Co-ordinators leave**: blame themselves for the failure of 'matches' and resign

* in the effort to make CA seem more natural, program co-ordinators **deny they are a program**. They don't tell people with disabilities that they are part of a CA program; don't evaluate or monitor advocacy
* **Any kind of formalisation or paper should be thrown out** as that makes citizen advocacy too much like a human service. (49)

For some Boards and co-ordinators, CAPE and the quest for the right way of doing citizen advocacy weigh very heavily. Some people simply get paralysed, especially when they have little experience of making matches so they can go wrong and people feel blamed. Productivity can be measured by the quantity rather than the inherent quality of matches.

As usual, Wolfensberger saw several additional difficulties. (50) 'CA could simply be seen as a stepping stone towards self advocacy rather than a process in its own right . . . It could easily get submerged by a mountain of volunteer programs which had few genuine similarities . . . CA projects could get trivialised into no more than sophisticated and expensive befriending schemes.' (51) De Ver highlighted how schemes in Britain tended to recruit informal and expressive advocates. These emphasised the social and leisure aspects but played down the more formal representative roles. (52) The popular video used to inform and train people about CA called 'Powerful Partnerships' by Avon CA shoots itself in the foot by over stressing the friendship aspects of advocacy and the close partnership, almost teamwork, with the various professionals. (53)

Yeadon commented: 'Because many young schemes in Britain have been pressured by the service system to produce results, one likely result is befriending.' (54) Wolfensberger warned again: 'If one looks at the publicity materials of CA offices, their slide shows, films and flyers, recruitment procedures, training content and methods, statistics, etc . . . one finds that what they have overwhelmingly tended to do is to emphasize informal rather than formal relationships.' (55)

At least one national scheme, one of the original founders of the Advocacy Alliance, makes a virtue of this 'difficulty'. One to One stresses the process of the relationship as opposed to the task of the advocacy. Friendship is the key concept to matching volunteers and people with disabilities. 'We should not be too purist about language. Debates in the advocacy movement assess the pros and cons of the word "volunteer" vis à vis "advocate" or "enabler". I feel it's what happens inside the relationship and their achievements that count. Advocacy will only happen if the two people involved know each other and trust each other. This trust is built up over time and through their relationship.' (56) Its north-west Surrey branch writes of 'liaising closely with day centres, group home and staff in Homewood Resource Centre'. (57) This seems a rather cosy link for an effective advocacy scheme.

RESEARCH

Research in the United States demonstrated a high degree of satisfaction with the advocacy role. There was a study of the personal and relationship characteristics of seventy-five advocate-protégé pairs involved in citizen advocacy in Vermont. All protégés were mentally retarded individuals living in the community . . . 'Higher levels of satisfaction were reported by advocates who more frequently provided interpersonal feedback, as opposed to instrumental support or assistance, and who more frequently engaged in mutual, community-based activities with protégés . . . satisfaction with advocacy relationships is more a function of what advocates and proteges do together than of their personal traits.' (58) 'A similar study of fifty-nine advocacy relationships in Melbourne, Australia over three years found prosaically that three characteristics of advocates which related to the maintenance of advocacy relationships, as well-being, flexibility and common sense.' (59)

A recent English study of twenty citizen advocates and ten people with learning difficulties found that 'advocates were helping their partners to challenge what services were doing in a range of areas including:-

*   inappropriate punishments
*   insensitive or inappropriate attempts to control behaviour
*   control over the partner's money
*   failure to involve the partner in making decisions
*   countering negative attitudes
*   concern about medication
*   preventing undesirable things happening
*   neglect.'

It is very difficult to imagine what an 'appropriate punishment' might be!

'Overall, the partners were very positive about the relationship with their advocates. They valued the latter's independence, their trustworthiness and their commitment. The advocates were seen as people who were prepared to listen and who shared leisure and social activities. In addition, some of the partners described advocates as providing practical help, and assistance both in achieving the partner's goals and in preventing undesirable things happening.' (60)

Such gains were rarely achieved without difficult struggles. 'Advocates were invariably refused information about their partner's medication on the grounds of confidentiality, even though the advocates were concerned that the drugs could be having bad side effects. One advocate reported that her partner seemed to be falling asleep all the time, though the staff didn't seem worried about it. Many advocates were suspicious that confidentiality was being used to cloak issues medical staff would rather not be questioned on . . . Many advocates have found the experience very traumatic'. (61)

A recent study of four projects in north Yorkshire suggests a valuable continuum of relationships from the 'soft' to the 'hard' end of advocacy practice. Possible roles ranged from *special friend, confidante, guide, mediator to trouble-shooter and lifeguard.* The study suggested that advocates in the mental health scheme were more often operating on the hard end of the scale, the complete reverse of the learning difficulties projects. Of 105 partnerships set up over two and a half years, fifty had ended. Half of these had met the objectives set; whilst the rest ended 'prematurely'. (62)

The Brighton advocacy project devastatingly questioned the whole nature of volunteer advocacy, especially in the mental health field. 'Although fashionable, terms such as "citizen's advocacy" and "self advocacy" are unhelpful, the former generally inferring a befriending process and the latter a combination of self - representation and collective advocacy. These are valuable spheres of activity, but they are not advocacy.' . . . 'In practice, we have discovered that the majority of service users are in fact largely satisfied with their care, but are often confused and frightened by the circumstances in which it occurs. The system can and does appear monolithic and all embracing to those within it. A principal issue within this is the role of volunteers. We had originally anticipated that the current situation, with myself as co-ordinator taking on the bulk of the casework, would be limited to a pilot stage. In practice, I have to say that the situations we have encountered, and the complexity of demands within them, make this seem unrealistic. In theory, there are very definite benefits in extending the casework role to volunteers working independently with follow up support. However, the time demands involved in training people up to that level, let alone in properly supporting workers involved in such tasks, make it unlikely that any great increase in efficiency of service delivery would result.' (63)

Carr painted almost as bleak a picture. She writes of the British flagship project: 'The recent CAPE of the Sheffield CA programme indicates that they still have only forty advocates, a third of whom are just good befriending relationships and Sheffield's only source of funding is from the providers of their local social services . . . Today there are roughly twenty programmes around the country which are either practising CA or are striving to develop initiatives into CA. Virtually all are experiencing difficulties with long term funding, many have less than twenty advocates. Because there are no basic rights to independent representation in law, there are many instances in which service staff in hospitals, hostels and private homes are denying access to advocates. Very often such staff claim to understand the need for advocacy, and claim to support the idea, but will insist that some voluntary visiting programme is already performing the function or, worse, that the staff are acting as advocates.' (64)

More worrying still is the continued exclusion of some minority groups. Despite the fact that service users from minority ethnic groups face a 'double discrimination', they are considerably under-represented both on management committees and as advocates and partners. (65) Simons notes that a Leeds organisation has appointed 'a black co-ordinator, co-opted black people onto the management committee and set out to recruit black and ethnic minority advocates'. (66) We have recently come across CA projects which excluded individuals living in residential care.

Wolfensberger commented on the tendency for projects to exclude the 'more impaired individuals'. Co-ordinators were caught up in the question of the 'degree of relationship reciprocity which the protege is capable or willing to offer. By this we mean that some people will not or cannot reciprocate socially or affectively. Take, for example, a man who had an accident and who had lain unconscious in a hospital for several years. His wife came so many times a week to hold his hand, but there had not been any relationship reciprocity in many years'. According to Wolfensberger, CA offices have tended to avoid non-reciprocal relationships and 'addressed themselves primarily to less impaired individuals'. (67)

ISSUES

CA still struggles to establish itself in Britain after more than thirteen years with much development and expenditure. It has proved almost impossible to find long-term sources of funding which are fully independent of service provision, such is the nature of our finances, dominated by health and social services departments. Tyne comments on Sheffield: 'There appears to be a severe "poverty trap" built into your agreement, such that as you develop alternative sources of funding, so the social services department grant will be reduced by an equivalent amount. You seem to be tied to the SSD for the foreseeable future.' (68) Initial dependence on trust money and 'Opportunities for Volunteering', both strictly time limited, has meant financial crises in many parts of the country, for example in York. Carr comments that a few CA groups have entered into agreements with NHS trusts or local authorities because of the difficulties in raising funds. (69)

It is clear from our visit to Georgia that CA flourishes more easily in the southern United States - the Bible Belt. Dowson suggests that advocates there are often motivated by a religious zeal to serve the community. Many citizen advocates are evangelical Christians who see themselves as involved in the joyful service of God. In this country, there is less of a tradition of Church support for secular community activity and more emphasis on internal activities. (70)

The research evidence indicates that a considerable proportion of matches are mainly if not completely based on friendships rather than on being more task centred. In the publications, there is a huge stress on the quality of relationships and considerably less on their efficacy. Very little work is done about the effectiveness or otherwise of the advocacy component. How much of what the partners ask for do the advocates really hear? How much of what they hear are they able to get? How effective are CA schemes compared with other schemes like professional advocacy?

The GLAD project dismissed CA as colluding with the 'handicappist structures of society'. Discussions with their young physically disabled users confirmed this analysis. They concluded that it was a very important concept 'yet without the necessary controls, could create yet another layer of dependency'. (71) Importantly the GLAD project was based from the start on discussions with disabled people, rather than on selling a specific set of ideologies and systems. It may be that the sort of zeal and evangelism inherent in CA is part of the problem.

CA seems to attract a high proportion of people who are currently or were formerly care staff. Over a third of the citizen advocates in the Bristol study had previously worked in the learning difficulties services. (72) In general, they may be staff who work in other localities so that conflict is minimal or may have moved on to different jobs or simply retired. This raises questions about their motivation. How far is the possible guilt about their own roles in services a factor? For example, the membership of MIND has an unusually large proportion of professionals, and guilt and frustration about existing roles and services are a major motivation. On the positive side, these particular advocates may know the detailed labyrinth in which their partners are enmeshed extremely well.

Dunning suggests a major conflict between two groups trying to claim overall ownership. The 'traditionalists' want to preserve the principles, and the 'service provisionists' who see advocacy as a means of promoting better quality services and increased user involvement. If either group dominates it would distort the essential purposes. He asks rather wider questions of ownership in considering the lack of disabled and ethnic minority representation on many CA Boards. The movement is staffed and managed by the 'unmarginalised: non-disabled, white, middle class people . . . few have been on the receiving end of services or could be said to have experienced significant disadvantage'.(73)

In some areas, there are already signs of a considerable adulteration of the CA principles, accompanied by a parallel trend to diversify to a more multi-component service. This can involve developing peer advocacy components; offering different sorts of advocacy, usually independent professionals. Ultimately these radical changes may reflect our different European culture more accurately and lead to the recruitment of many more genuine volunteer advocates.

References

(1) Alan Tyne 'A report on an Evaluation of Sheffield Citizen Advocacy' Sheffield Citizen Advocacy and National Development Team 1991
(2) Kate Butler, Sally Carr and Frances Sullivan 'Citizen Advocacy: a powerful partnership' National Citizen Advocacy 1988 (Pge 3)
(3) National Citizen Advocacy: September 1993
(4) Wolf Wolfensberger 'A Multi-component advocacy/protection Schema' CAMR 1977
(5) Wolf Wolfensberger 'Towards Citizen Advocacy for the Handicapped, impaired and disadvantaged' Nebraska Psychiatric Institute 1971
(6) National Association for Retarded Citizens 'Avenues to Change: implementation of citizen advocacy through state and local ARCs' (Book 2) N.A.R.C. 1974

(7) M. Addison 'Some problems regarding citizen advocacy' in G. J. Bensberg and C. Rude (editors) 'Advocacy Systems for Developmentally Disabled Adults' Texas Tech University Press, 1977

(8) Bob Sang and John O'Brien 'Advocacy: the UK and American experiences' Kings Fund 1984

(9) David Brandon 'Innovation without Change?' MacMillan 1991

(10) Advocacy Alliance 'Guidelines for One-to-One Advocacy in Mental Handicap Hospitals' November 1984

(11) Amanda Forrest 'Including the Excluded' Sheffield Citizen Advocacy, 1986

(12) John O'Brien 'Learning from Citizen Advocacy Programs' Georgia Advocacy Office, Georgia, USA, 1981)

(13) Kate Butler et al. (Pge 1)

(14) Kate Butler et al. (Pge 40)

(15) Sally Carr 'Personal Communication' November 1993

(16) National Citizen Advocacy Annual Report 1990/91, NCA 1991, (P4)

(17) John O'Brien 'Building Creative Tension - the development of a citizen advocacy program for people with mental handicaps' Georgia Advocacy Office, U.S.A. 1982 (Pge 14)

(18) Kate Butler et al. (Pge 5)

(19) Wolf Wolfensberger 'Voluntary Associations on Behalf of Societally Devalued People and/or Handicapped People', Toronto, NIMR 1984

(20) NCA Newsletter, October 1993

(21) Working Party on a code of practice for citizen advocacy with older people - notes of a meeting at NCA November 1993 and see also 'Advocacy - voicing the wishes of the older person' Age Concern, November 1989

(22) Alison Wertheimer 'Speaking Out: citizen advocacy and older people' Centre for Policy on Ageing 1993 (Pge 20)

(23) Sally Carr Personal Communication November 1993

(24) Alison Wertheimer Ibid.

(25) Beth Johnson Foundation 'Advocacy in Action', Spring/Summer 1993.

(26) Barbara Avila 'Advocacy Scheme report' Camden Age Concern February 1993

(27) Barbara Avila 'Old People and Advocacy' in 'Speaking Out for Advocacy' Labyrinth 1994

(28) Barbara Avila 'Annual report on Advocacy at Ingestre Road Elderly Person's Home' Camden Age Concern, October 1993 and see also an account of the Cheltenham CA scheme for elderly people in "Advocacy - voicing the wishes of the older person' Age Concern, November 1989 (Pge 11)

(29) Bob Peckford, Director of Advocacy Services, British Deaf Association, Advocacy Conference, April 1994, Manchester

(30) Christopher Reid 'Deaf Citizens in Partnership' RNID 1994

(31) Angie Lee 'Sense' 11-13 Clifton Terrace, London, N4 3SR

(32) Camberwell Advocacy Office: personal communication: Kathy West - Co-ordinator: 1 February 1994

(33) Emma Fowler 'Kingston Advocacy Group' Information Pack 1993

(34) Sally Carr 'The Development of CA in the UK' paper given at the Citizen Advocacy World Congress in Lincoln, Nebraska, USA, October 1990 and see also Wolfensberger's reference to crisis citizen advocacy in 'A Multi-component advocacy/protection Schema' CAMR 1977, (Pge 5)

(35) Sally Carr Personal Communication November 1993 and also in Barbara Webb and Lesley Holly 'Evaluating a Citizen Advocacy Scheme' Findings, Social Care Research, Rowntree Foundation, June 1994 on crisis advocates

(36) 'Crisis Advocacy' in Llais 31, Winter 1994 (Pge 28)

(37) See for example the robustly defensive section by Wolfensberger on 'Outright perversions of normalization' in R. J. Flynn and K. E. Nitsch (Editors) in 'Normalization, Social Integration and Community Services' University Park Press, Baltimore 1980 and also his lecture 'Citizen Advocacy Principles and Perversions' World Citizen Advocacy Congress, Lincoln, Nebraska, 6 October 1990

(38) John O'Brien and Wolf Wolfensberger 'CAPE - Standards for Citizen Advocacy Program Evaluation' NIMR Toronto, 1979

(39) Ken Simons 'Citizen Advocacy: the inside view' Norah Fry research centre, 1993 (Pge 31)

(40) See for example Wolf Wolfensberger 'The Principle of Normalisation' NIMR 1971

(41) L. Baucom (Editor) 'Citizen Advocacy - how to make it happen' 1980 and C.D. Rude (Editor) 'Action through Advocacy. A Manual for training volunteers' 1980 and Texas Technical University 'Citizen Advocacy Resources' 1979, all Lubbock, Texas: Research and Training Center in Mental Retardation

(42) John O'Brien 'Learning from Citizen Advocacy' Programs' Georgia Advocacy Office, 1987

(43) Nan Carle 'Key Concepts (5) Citizen Advocacy' CMH 1980

(44) Kathy Alexander 'The Forum as a Safeguard of Citizen Advocacy and a Protection against the Dangers of Isolation' Citizen Advocacy Forum (USA), vol. Two, number One, November 1991

(45) Vince Molloy 'Citizen Advocacy in Practice' Citizen Advocacy Forum, November 1991

(46) Vince Molloy Values into Action newsletter: Summer 1993

(47) VIA newsletter: summer 1993

(48) Mary Tanguay 'Citizen Advocacy: strategies for addressing human service needs in the community' Canada's Mental Health, March 1987

(49) Carolyn Bardwell Wheeler 'Separating Effective Practice from Principles' Citizen Advocacy Forum, Nov. 1991

(50) Wolf Wolfensberger 'Reflections on the Status of CA' National Institute for Mental Retardation (Toronto, Canada) and the Georgia Advocacy Office, 1983 (Pge 7)

(51) Series of lectures on Advocacy given by Wolf Wolfensberger in Lytham St Annes, Lancashire, September 1987

(52) J. Lyne de Ver 'Citizen Advocacy: a report to the Gwent Joint Planning Forum' 1987

(53) Avon Citizen Advocacy 'Powerful Partnerships' 1989

(54) Clive Yeadon 'Some implications for citizen advocacy in a changing welfare state' paper given to the World Citizen Advocacy Congress, Lincoln, Nebraska: 7 October 1990

(55) Wolf Wolfensberger 'Reflections on the Status of Citizen Advocacy' National Institute on Mental Retardation, Canada 1983 (Pges 9-11)

(56) One to One 'People's Lives' One to One 1994

(57) Maureen Rutter 'One to One' in 'Speaking Out for Advocacy - a report of the National Conference' Labyrinth 1994

(58) Gary C. Widrick *et al.* 'Citizen Advocacy Relationships: Advocate, Protégé, and Relationships Characteristics and Satisfaction Ratings' Journal of the Association for Persons with Severe Handicaps, Vol. 15, No 3, Pges 170-176, 1990

(59) P. O'Brien *et al* . 'Personality characteristics of Advocates and Maintenance of Relationships in a Citizen Advocacy Programme' The British Journal of Mental Subnormality, vol. XXXVIII, Part 1, January 1992, No 74 (Pges 24-31)

(60) Ken Simons 'Citizen Advocacy: the inside view' Norah Fry research centre, 1993 (pge 78)

(61) Lynn Eaton 'Pleading the case for Advocates' Search 18, Winter 1993/4 (Pges 14-16)

(62) Barabara Webb and Lesley Holly 'Evaluating a Citizen Advocacy Scheme' in Findings: Social Care Research 52, Rowntree Foundation, June 1994

(63) MIND in Brighton and Hove 'The Advocacy Project in Adult Mental Health Services' report for the period February 1991 - February 1992

(64) Sally Carr 'The Development of CA in the UK' paper given at the Citizen Advocacy World Congress in Lincoln, Nebraska, USA, October 1990

(65) Carol Baxter 'Issues and Services for People with Learning Disabilities from Black and Ethnic Minority Communities' Kings Fund 1992 (Pge 142)

(66) Quoted in Ken Simons 'Citizen Advocacy: the inside view' Norah Fry research centre, 1993 (Pge 43)

(67) Wolf Wolfensberger 'Reflections on the Status of Citizen Advocacy' National Institute on Mental Retardation, Canada 1983

(68) Alan Tyne 'A report on an evaluation of Sheffield Citizen Advocacy' Ibid (Pge 20) 1991

(69) Sally Carr Personal Communication: 6 September 1994

(70) Steve Dowson Personal communication: 3 August 1994

(71) Jacqui Christie 'Speaking for Ourselves' GLAD 1993 (Appendix III)

(72) Ibid. Ken Simons (Pge 42)

(73) Andrew Dunning 'Who owns citizen advocacy?' paper given at the Caring for Elderly in the Community conference, University of Plymouth, April 1993

SEVEN: PEER ADVOCACY

"It takes a man that has the blues to sing the blues'
Leadbelly quoted in Alan Lomax
'The Land where the Blues began' Methuen 1993

LINKS

Unlike citizen advocacy, peer advocacy doesn't come with sophisticated packaging, volumes on development and training and a persistent struggle to preserve purity. In most areas it is relatively new, appearing in none of the current major advocacy texts; but in some ways it has a distinguished lineage. (1) John Perceval, himself a former long stay psychiatric patient, founded the 'Alleged Lunatic's Friends Society' in 1845. Four years earlier, he had acted as a peer advocate for Dr Pearce, a patient in the criminal section of Bethlehem Hospital. (2)

Much earlier, in the sixteenth century, Timothy Rogers, a nonconformist Minister, who had a nervous breakdown in his early twenties, published a pamphlet called 'Advices to Friends of Melancholly People' which stressed the personal experience of depression in the helping of others. 'It is impossible to understand the nature of it in any other way than by Experience . . . Look at those with Melancholly with pity and compassion . . . Do not attribute the effects of the Disease to the Devil. . . Tell them of others who have been in such Anguish, and under such a terrible Distemper, and yet have been delivered.' He was describing the importance of what is now called 'positive role models', still insufficiently appreciated. (4)

Peer advocacy is linked with peer support. Alcoholics Anonymous, the largest self-help organisation in the world formed at the turn of the century, supports hundreds of thousands of alcoholics and through the sponsors provides some individual help as well. Sponsors can have a sort of peer advocacy role, for example, in interceding with aggrieved employers. (3)

Mentoring is also increasingly common. The term derives from Mentor, the revered adviser to the young Telemachus in Homer's Odyssey. (5) It means a role model, coach and confidant - someone who knows how it is from their own personal experience. Jeoff Thompson, former world karate champion, mentors Darren Campbell would-be Olympic sprinter. He comments 'Darren has the desire, the smile and he does the hard work. I ensure that he doesn't make the mistakes I made. The mentor scheme's objective is to show that sportspeople can take care of themselves and recycle their talents back into the community.' (6)

There are a number of examples of these innovative processes within the services. The Swansea Prison Listener scheme, based on American prison buddy systems, started in August 1991, trains fellow prisoners to counsel depressed and suicidal colleagues. Individual prisoners are selected for their maturity, knowledge of the system and a genuine desire to help others. These 'peer counsellors' are trained by the Samaritans who provide support and supervision in the confidential weekly discussions. It seems to work well. (7)

Patients admitted to the San Francisco General Hospital are also provided with peer counsellors - someone suffering from mental distress and with experience of in-patient treatment. The peer counsellor's task is to humanise the hospital environment by offering advice and information which are different from the professional hospital treatment. (8) The Beth Johnson Foundation in Stoke-on-Trent trains senior citizens as peer health counsellors 'to help their peers towards positive health and well being'. (9)

PEERS

Brian Stocker spent 14 years as a patient in a long stay mental handicap hospital. Now he is a peer advocate, helping people move out . 'Because I've been in hospital, I know how people feel when they get into the community . . . There are still a lot of people who are very unhappy and things build up inside them. There'll be a lot of pressure on those people when they move into the community and some will draw themselves in more and won't talk. You have to be patient with them, sit down and try to understand. I can help them. I can find out what services they want. If they're scared to go out, I can go out with them . . . They need people like us to talk to.' (10)

Advocacy in Action is a well known Nottingham based project for people with learning difficulties, involved in peer support and advocacy. It is a workers collective and small community business set up by a group of disabled people in partnership with non-disabled people, based on the idea of mutual help and support. Their firm belief is that it is best for disabled people to represent one another. They turn the experience of being disabled into something which is valued and appreciated. "We are the experts in our own lives." They emphasise education, contributing to social work courses and challenging paternalistic and ablist ideas. (11)

The Spinal Injuries Association (SIA) provides a Link Scheme which is 'one of its oldest and most successful services to members.'

The scheme is based on the idea that the best way both full and associate SIA members can help each other is by getting in touch and sharing. (12) Members can share experiences of services, practical aids, access to the social security maze . . .

In general, peer advocacy involves individual support by recovering or recovered users in helping other service users to express and fulfil their individual wishes. (13) It differs from conventional citizen advocacy, described earlier, in that advocates are not so called 'valued persons' but people who are also survivors of the system. They share the social stigmatisation of what Goffman calls the 'spoiled identity' of those they support. (14) It is one way of holding the whole process of social valuing and devaluing up against a strong light.

The development of peer support and advocacy counteracts negative processes and helps users to see both themselves and their experiences in a much more positive light. It accepts that they are valuable people with useful experiences. They can be both advocates and also colleagues of mental health professionals. They can be taken seriously, learn increased skills, and receive respect from powerful others. But the essential test is whether peer advocacy is 'effective' and has both distinctive and positive features.

Peter Campbell, of Survivors Speak Out, describes one incident in his long experience of peer advocacy. 'I have used the mental health system for twenty-five years, and I am pretty articulate and know fairly well the ins and outs of the system. Last autumn when I was on Section 3 (compulsory detention) for a month and was in an acute ward in London, I had a friend of mine, a fellow user, acting as my advocate. It was the first time . . . and it made a really big difference to me. She spoke on my behalf and supported me and it transformed the nature of that meeting. It was quite a learning experience for the other people and the mental health workers. All I can say is that it made a real difference to my feelings of empowerment.'

'She was someone who was in complete sympathy/ empathy with me. She knew the "power trip" from the inside. It was "inside" her too. She was emotionally involved which I saw as a plus. We were reciprocally involved. I expected that I would act as her advocate at some point. This strengthened us both vis-à-vis the system. That reciprocity establishes a particular bond with a potential for deeper benefits. For example, it made a difference for me that this peer advocacy had grown out of friendship. The solidarity issue means that there is a "piquancy" when the advocacy relationship is clearly connected to a common and clear approach to wider issues. She was realistic. She had an instinctive knowledge of what was on and what was not on. She was aware of the essential limits of advocacy and of my powerlessness from her direct experience.' (15)

Campbell describes an exciting and stimulating process. He felt both invigorated and empowered in a way which could hardly have been achieved by a 'straight' advocate. He felt that his particular plight was appreciated from the inside. That appreciation was closely linked with a friendship not 'befriending' which was reciprocal. There might come a time and situation when the tables might be turned and he would advocate for her.

Writing of both self-and peer advocacy and racism, Shuresh Patel, a mental health service survivor developing patient's councils in central Lancashire, found that 'staff ridiculed my ideas about advocacy; also there was a resistance from other patients who felt overwhelmed by the power of the staff. If patients don't assert their rights, they will just get walked over by the psychiatric system. Discussions involving staff met with hostility: some staff were actually disgusted. For example, some referred to the embryonic patient's council as a "witch hunt".'

'In taking up allegations of racism in a psychiatric setting, I was always told that it was just my delusions. I was allegedly hearing things in my head. But on one occasion I had a witness. I was called a 'Pakki' by a hospital staff member. I complained and he got disciplined. I have just given up my job in Unravel Mills, an industrial therapy unit. It's just an extended mental institution in the community. Packing things into boxes was humiliating and there was also no heating in the part of the building where I worked. I made friends with the only other coloured user who complained he couldn't get a vegetarian meal, necessary on religious grounds. I served as his advocate. The staff responded "He should change his religion". Like me he was a Hindu and we were both supposed to change to Christianity to solve the menu problem! Their whole attitude was very hostile.' (16)

When Perceval mounted a systematic assault on conditions in Northampton County asylum, where the poet John Clare had been incarcerated for many years, he faced similar resistances. He was attacked by a hospital official, commenting in a local newspaper that Perceval's 'sympathies with the insane are of a very morbid character and his judgement to the last feeble and weak'. (17) This attack attempted to re-clientise him.

Karen Campbell, like Perceval with user experience but more recently, writes of her work in Fulbourn Hospital, Cambridge: 'On a

106

ward level, complaints can get ignored, or false assurances given that the matter is being dealt with, when in fact it is being ignored or buried. Similarly, buckpassing such as "That is not our responsibility . . . we have no say on that . . ." also occurs. Lack of information, refusal to make information available or denying any knowledge of means of access to information can be a problem'.

'The most blatant form of obstructionism our (peer) advocates have met with is staff apathy and indifference; staff failing to inform users that the advocates will be visiting the ward and that they are available on a regular basis. Staff can feel threatened and undermined by "patients" operating outside their usual roles, and in what they perceive, as quasi staff roles. When people have been defined as unskilled and inferior, it is usually difficult to accept them in more equal and skilled roles.' (18)

Peer advocates also faced major problems in Hillend Hospital, St Albans. Three people went on the wards to act as advocates with the staff. What they faced was tricks, trade-offs, manipulations and exploitations from staff who were improperly trained and not advised about advocacy and empowerment. In the end, the advocates were excluded from the wards. The St Albans Users and Advocacy Group 'learned not to trust staff'. (19)

Some citizen advocacy projects now recruit users as advocates. The three-year 'Deaf Citizens in Partnership' project recruited deaf people to advocate for deaf people. ' . . . the experience of one partnership (which lasted for six months) provided an insight into the potential for a relationship between deaf advocate and partner. It is doubtful whether a hearing advocate could have achieved similar benefits for the partner. The partner's and advocate's experiences of being deaf linked them together. It is not certain that a hearing advocate could achieve a similar effect. Deaf advocates will, in many cases, naturally empathise with the partner's concerns and wishes, and help to increase his/her self-worth through befriending and by introducing their partner to other deaf people'.(20)

The Birmingham Citizen Advocacy Project set up in 1987 by the local association for Mental Health, grew out of a consultation exercise with mental health users, stressing the need for advocacy. Initially based in a south Birmingham psychiatric hospital, a particularly unsuitable location, it received funding for three years. Lorraine Lewis, currently a user of mental health services, was appointed as co-ordinator in February 1990 and the office moved to the Community Enterprise centre.

Lorraine saw advocacy as a fundamentally anti-discriminatory activity. They deliberately set aside the traditional 'valued citizen' condition. They saw a potential advocate as 'anybody who can make things happen'. They gave considerable support to the matches between the advocate and the partner. Fifty percent were peer advocates, meaning that both partners have or had direct experiences of the mental health services. Lorraine had a very extensive network in Birmingham, particularly amongst users, so that new advocates with mental health backgrounds were coming forward all the time.

Bernard has had experience of psychiatric treatment. He feels peer advocates are best. "Bali understands my problems because she's been through similar crap. She doesn't see herself as an advocate and me as the partner. We share a deep care and concern for each other which is both equal and reciprocal." He and Bali have developed a self advocacy group based on the Soho psychiatric day centre and edit 'The Pioneer Voice' a mental health users magazine.

Lorraine sees the practice of equality as vital in advocacy. She encourages reciprocity and the sharing of personal stories and other experiences. She agrees with Bernard that it often improves matches where both people have a mental health problem. "Many things just don't have to be explained. There is an increased intuitive understanding when someone has been through a similar process ." (21)

Peer advocacy can be very diverse. It may involve 'wounded staff' taking up in their spare time issues on behalf of people they identify with. It may also involve long term friendships between people on a reasonably equal footing where both may have an advocacy role for each other at different times. Peers may represent each other at formal case conferences when it is difficult to speak out on behalf of yourself and where the survivor feels under considerable pressure from the professionals. Peer advocacy can come less equally from more experienced peers who act like mentors, with some training in representation and whose life is more together, at least at that moment.

FUTURE

What is the future for peer advocacy? Can it be developed and extended without being dominated by the various professionals? That could be a difficult journey. Can peer advocates be supported and trained without becoming pseudo professionals? Can they provide effective advocacy and how is that to be measured? Can they receive respect from the professionals - perceived as colleagues and equals and at the same time being essentially challenging? Health and social services staff are full of fear. People easily get defensive and angry.

In most peer support and advocacy schemes, there is already considerable control by professionals. Some resemble 'star prisoner' systems where 'trusties' are given special status and privileges. Their training, relationships and structures are dominated by the needs of professionals. Peter Campbell asks questions. 'Is there a way to provide the necessary support for peer support without some sort of professionalised take over? What are the tensions between formal and informal structures? What will the role be for activists who are very critical of systemised care? The best support comes from friendship. It is shared one to one support during the wobbly periods. Some people's networks are already dominated by survivors. Survivors have similar experiences and backgrounds. Is that feeling of common experiences real? In a way there is a legend of collective experience when people's experiences of distress and service use may be, in reality, extremely different.' (22) As the survivors movements develop, schisms are inevitable. Groups will increasingly stress differences rather than commonalities.

Peer advocacy could help promote a number of changes in the mental health services. It could help staff to appreciate that service users have relevant and valuable experiences, gifts and skills. It could help speaking out, gradually changing the suffocating environment of passivity. Service users could become, at the very least, more active partners in their recovery. Peer advocacy challenges the whole negative process of 'mentalism', particularly in staff and carers. (23) When seen increasingly as people of value, with something important to contribute, it is easier for users to come in from the margins. They can more easily be perceived as unique and valued individuals.

Peer advocacy would offer individual help and friendship to users in contrast or in addition to the mostly groupwork of self-help. It would require considerable changes in staff attitudes; changes in relevant structures; much support and some training in specific areas like welfare rights, practical counselling and listening skills as well as in advocacy. Training would supplement their already extensive direct knowledge and personal qualities rather than turn them into substitutes for professionals.

TRAINING

Advocate's training needs will vary greatly. They may need help in listening skills and also in being assertive. They may need to understand more of the labyrinth of services and what the various professionals do. They may need more particular help, for example, in understanding the side effects of various drugs prescribed or ways of accessing children to mainstream education. Most training needs will be specific to the experiences and needs of the person they support.

Birmingham C.A. training strongly challenges existing stereotypes of psychiatric illness. They look at areas of 'mentalism'; the development of negative imagery from films like 'Psycho', radio and magazines and the newspapers. They examine negative attitudes induced by professional training; feelings that professionals are 'superior beings', reinforced by ten thousand things inside the services, everything from the ward round to the staff offices.

In their view, training can only be done by those with a direct experience of disability. That experience of both suffering and treatment is essential to understanding oppression at any depth. One report points this out clearly: 'Only those who experience disability as a form of social oppression really understand thoroughly enough to teach about its reality. It was decided by the Trainers Forum that training around disability should only be carried out by disabled people, equipped with professional training techniques and a thorough understanding of all disabled people's lifestyles within the context of a social model theory of disability.' (24)

'Objectives of a course:
* to reach a social model of disability as opposed to an individual, medical model
* challenge some of the common myths and false distinctions
* demonstrate practical application of equal opportunities
* recognise that black disabled people, disabled women, disabled lesbians and gays experience multiple oppression
* to draft action plan for constructive changes
* equip participants with a working knowledge of disability which will enable them to recognise discriminatory language and stereotypical visual images.' (25)

The Birmingham CA project confronts 'mentalism', discrimination against those with mental illness, head on. Each new advocate gets a training pack and works with the co-ordinator on three basic sections. The first section defines what a mental health problem is in a valued way. What is society's response? What are the basic needs? The second defines different types of advocacy; its history and basic principles; who needs it and who does it; what are the various roles of a citizen advocate? It looks at various conflicts and pressures. What to expect from the Citizen Advocacy Office. Why do people need advocates? The various roles of service providers. Who are advocates ? What do they do ? The sorts of needs advocates can meet. The third is much more challenging. New advocates are given four scenarios to work on by themselves. They have to write their gut reaction to each story, working through their written comments with the co-ordinator. This encourages them to look more deeply at themselves and their attitudes, some may be negative. Service users must also examine their own social negatives about mental illness. (26)

CHANGING SERVICES

Conlan suggests some elements for a 'code of practice:

* Peer advocates will only act or speak on users' behalf as the user wishes.
* they will support people when they speak for themselves
* they will act ethically and behave towards people with honesty, courtesy, discretion, respect for their dignity, confidentiality and privacy
* they will not mix socially with managers or other professionals
* they are accountable to the people who use their services
* they should make no decisions or choices on behalf of the person.. . ' (27)

It is difficult to see how these very commendable aims are going to have any reality without a relevant structure to encourage and enforce them.

It is no good designing more three pin plugs if there are no appropriate power points for them. Advocates battle for a better deal for service users. Unless they are simply to get ulcers, they must connect with sensitive service systems which fully appreciate their function or, at the very least, one which is not actively hostile. Services must develop ways of seeing feedback, often very critical, as useful and even important. Accepting criticism with good grace is an important and extremely rare skill. Advocates often pay a huge personal cost for the role they play.

Peer advocates need formal ways of taking up issues. (28) They need easy and relaxed access to senior managers who can make the real changes; appropriate recognition and respect from relevant professionals and even support; a melting of traditionally defensive attitudes; as well as formal complaints procedures which work. In most of these areas, we have still much to learn from our colleagues in the Netherlands. (29)

Some of the peer advocacy movement will need more formal systems as well as organisation. It is much too valuable a process just to be left to a few dedicated professionals or services who just happen to know someone who. . . The organisation should be local and composed exclusively of people who have had experience of mental health services, except for some sympathetic supporters and advisers, who can provide relevant expertise - like lawyers and accountants. Such formal organisations bring many problems, already experienced in the citizen advocacy movement. It may stifle natural friendships; it may drift away from the formal advocacy towards informal befriending. It may tend to suffocate in petty bureaucracy, death through a million inflexible rules.

Not everyone who is a service user is necessarily a suitable advocate. Some people may be too introverted, lack passion and not have the assertion skills, just like some of the rest of the population. A major test must be their efficacy as advocates. Mostly, the needs of the survivor will dictate the nature of the advocacy. Does this particular person have the passion, skills and discipline to get a better deal for current service users? Sometimes the answer will be no. Co-ordinators will have to exclude some people as well as encourage others.

The schemes would offer one to one volunteers, both people having in common a direct experience of disability and the services. Paid co-ordinators, also with an experience of using services, would identify people in need of advocacy. They would recruit individual advocates with relevant experience and skills. They would also make the introductions and develop the matches. Part of the matching might lie in the similarity of experiences of the services and their 'treatment'. The co-ordinators would provide a bank of information for the use of the advocates and provide information about relevant workshops. Advocates could meet with others to share both their triumphs and disasters.

Peer advocates will need considerable support, to see the world through the eyes of the other. Coming into this kind of advocacy could involve them in fierce struggles with former enemies and re- awaken old and personal battles, particularly about medication and ECT. They must avoid fighting their own struggles at the expense of the person being supported. Advocates are ordinary human beings. They may over identify, fail to appreciate fully the differences between the person they are supporting and their own situation. They may sexually and financially exploit their partners. Just because you've tried to kill yourself or sit in a wheelchair doesn't mean you necessarily understand what is going through the head of another individual in an apparently similar situation.

I (the author) have wrestled with the dilemmas of advocacy for fellow mental health service users, both inside and outside MIND. Often I had the more formal paid role of a social worker or MIND regional Director, acting on behalf of patients. Such advocacy roles were frequently extremely difficult. For example, it was usually made difficult to get access to records and other written material, readily available in the social work role. I was sometimes resented personally and seen as betraying my colleagues. I was perceived as a deviant member of the established club who had gone over the wall. As a professional, you were presumed to have made some kind of choice, to be reliable and, above all, to be loyal, to share an unquestioned faith in colleagues, at least publicly. Choosing to be on the side of the users was to make both a deviant and disloyal decision.

I had made no secret of my experience of psychiatric treatment, writing about it in various books and professional journals. Colleagues would comment on that experience as an explanation for my subsequently perceived deviant behaviour. My unusual interest in the experiences of users would be explained in terms of individual deviancy. One particular psychiatrist talked openly of me 'going native' in a hospital case conference. Another talked of me being 'untrustworthy'.

When more obviously involved in peer advocacy, I was perceived as 'crossing boundaries', of 'getting emotionally over-involved', of 'letting my passions rule my head', of 'over identifying with clients and patients'. A charge nurse told me that it was harmful to tell users that I had been in their situation. "It blurs professional/patient boundaries. You should save that sort of communication for your own psychotherapy sessions. You shouldn't bring it into the work". It was suggested in various letters from professionals that my peer advocacy was a result of my instability and, a more subtle assault, 'actually working against the best interests of the patients concerned'. I had apparently ' lost all objectivity'.

Certain patients were being 'penalised' because of my damaging support.

I recall representing some patients on a long stay hospital ward and talking to both them and other professionals about some of their experiences as being similar to my own. A nurse said to me during a coffee break: 'Remember David, they're only mental patients. They complain about conditions and you represent them. But they don't really understand things in the way you and I both do. Their decision making processes are permanently damaged. Don't ever confuse their situation with your own. We go home at the end of every day and they stay right here. They don't have our helicopter view of the world. They don't have either our education or professional discipline.' Nobody has any helicopter view of the world. We all walk on the earth. This nurse was seriously deluded.

Peer advocates will need the kind of passionate and yet thoughtful support which the Birmingham CA service offers. They may also need advice from sympathetic professionals, both inside and outside the relevant services, to redress some of the immense power imbalances. The advocacy organisation will need an advisory board composed of people with specific skills and expertise. This skill and knowledge could be called on whenever needed.

The core of this support would come from a local committee of other users. Those without direct experience of disability would be excluded or serve on the various advisory committees. The core group would work on their common experiences and support to those now in similar situations. This emphasis on the common experience of oppression and distress would provide a strong ballast for the advocacy movement.

ISSUES

Peer advocacy could be an important element in the overall struggle to include rather than exclude people from mainstream society. It involves a form of judo which begins to value those qualities which were until only recently both devalued and dismissed. We have tens of thousands of people who have had an experience of considerable importance and relevance - of having some form of disability. We could facilitate their creative use of these experiences.

It could be a crucial element in "rites of passage" such as Alcoholics Anonymous provides for some alcoholics, to find useful expressions for a hitherto devalued experience. For example, our society offers no valued transition from so-called insanity to sanity.

Estroff argues that there is no socially acceptable alternative to mental patienthood. 'The sorts of roles, expectations, stereotypes and responses that are fashioned around long-term psychiatric patients in the community are not markedly different from those that accompany the back-ward patient in the mental hospital. Not only do we view them as unintegrated within the community but we isolate them by constantly reminding them of their incompetencies, and by introducing them to peers with whom they may be more comfortable.' (30)

'Even where participants might be said to have got better their credibility was easily put into question. At best they had a precarious foothold in ordinary life in which their personhood was constantly on probation and they were required to provide repeated demonstrations that they were normal . . . their potential as human beings capable of giving as much as receiving was generally disregarded.' (31) Perring makes a similar point in a more recent study of mental health service users leaving Claybury and Friern Hospitals. 'People's status is not restored by their return to the community.' (32)

Reissman envisages a consumer-centred model of services for the 1990s that calls for a restructuring of help so that those who ordinarily receive it can function as producers. 'Self help groups, peer helping and self care are prime illustrations of this model.' (33) Peter Campbell comments: 'We are encouraged to be victims, to look vertically to experts for the solution to problems they have defined, rather than to reach out for those around us who have a shared experience.' (34)

The peer support movement must be careful to include some of the most marginalised people, the poor and homeless, as well as those who are black and female. Sayal comments: 'It is my belief that there is an indissoluble link between the politics of racial oppression and its psychological effects on black women. . . The use of psychiatry as a method of control and punishment of black people is on the increase and there is more encroachment of psychiatric expertise into prisons and courtrooms.' (35) Racism is a particular and difficult problem within the special hospital psychiatric system where significant numbers of staff have links with the National Front. 'The culture at the Ashworth hospital nurtures covert and fosters racism.' (36)

We have no idea how effective the advocacy of peers might be. It is possible that peers are so devalued in the eyes of staff and other powerful stakeholders that the whole attempt will backfire on the unfortunate service user. It may be that the re-clientisation discussed earlier is inevitable in many services. We need to consider that as a pessimistic possibility. There is evidence from Rippere's study that some staff are given a hard time when returning to psychiatric work after mental illness. (37) Staff will also need help in accepting not only the process of advocacy, but also some unusual advocates.

The problems will vary in degree and severity in the different disability groups. For example, stigma seems to vary from group to group. Advocates with a background of long-term mental illness or learning difficulties will usually be more devalued than those with a physical disability. As we have seen, there may be considerable communication advantages in being represented by someone who is also deaf rather than someone who is hearing. The same advantages may occur when the advocate has the same native language and culture as the service user who has, for example, no English.

How can structures be developed which support effectively; ensure the quality of the advocacy; reduce considerably the risk of exploitation - but don't crush this whole, delicate process? Dowson suggests pessimistically that the newer systems tend to copy the repressive patterns of the old service systems and run into the same sorts of bureaucratic problems. (38)

References

(1) See for example David Brandon 'Peer Supporters could act as wounded healers' Social Work Today, 14 May 1992

(2) David Brandon 'Innovation without Change? - consumer power in psychiatric services' MacMillan1991 (Pge 19)

(3) Richard Hunter and Ida MacAlpine 'Three Hundred Years of Psychiatry - 153 -1860' Oxford Univ. Press, 1963 (Pge 358)

(4) Alcoholics Anonymous 'Questions & Answers on Sponsorship - 1983' see 'Should a sponsor intercede with an employer?' (Pge 20)

(5) Mentoring is also mentioned in John O'Brien 'Learning from Citizen Advocacy Programs' Georgia Advocacy Office, 1987 (Pge 5)

(6) Richard Liston 'Campbell on the track of Glory' The Observer 17 January 1993

(7) Brian Davies Senior Probation Officer, Swansea Prison 'Swansea Listener Scheme' unpublished 1992 and see a similar scheme in Saughton Prison, Edinburgh 'These men are all killers... now they have devoted their lives to saving their cellmates' Daily Mirror 26 August 1994 (Pges 2-3)

(8) Kathryn Church and David Revell 'User involvement in mental health services in Canada' in 'Report of Common Concerns: International conference of user involvement in mental health services' MIND 1990 and also Richard Warner chapter five 'Creative Programming' (Pge 128) in Shula Ramon (Editor) 'Beyond Community Care - normalisation and integration work' MacMillan 1991

(9) Beth Johnson Foundation 'Peer Health Counselling' Parkfield House, 64 Princes Road, Stoke-on-Trent

(10) Elinor Harbridge 'Why not listen to the real professionals?' Community Living January 1993

(11) A visit to Advocacy in Action, Nottingham, February 1994

(12) 'Link Scheme Relaunch' Spinal Injuries Association no 70, September 1993 (Pge 1)

(13) David Brandon 'Peer supporters could act as wounded healers' Social Work Today 14 May 1992 (Pge 25)

(14) Peter Campbell Personal Communication June 1992

(15) Erving Goffman 'Asylums - essays on the social situation of mental patients and other inmates' Penguin 1968

(16) Shuresh Patel Personal Communication January 1993

(17) Quoted in Edward M. Podvoll 'The Seduction of Madness' Century 1990 (Pge 57)

(18) Karen Campbell Personal Communication December 1992

(19) Mary Jo Joyce 'St Albans Users and Advocacy Group' in John Black (Editor) 'Forging Our Future - conference report' Northampton, 18 March 1994

(20) Christopher Reid 'Deaf Citizens in Partnership' RNID 1994 (Pge 16)

(21) Visit to Birmingham Citizen Advocacy Project, Summer 1992

(22) Peter Campbell Personal communication September 1992

(23) See the specific discrimination material in 'MINDs policy paper on user involvement' MIND 1991

(24) K. Gillespie-Sells and J. Campbell 'Disability Equality Training: Trainers Guide' CCETSW June 1991 (Pge 7)

(25) Ibid. (Pge 23)

(26) Visit to Birmingham Citizen Advocacy Project, Summer 1992

(27) Edna Conlan 'Peer Advocacy in Mental Health' in Advocacy Code of Practice - recommendations' UK. Advocacy Network, 1994 (Pges 5-6)

(28) See for example Peter Beresford and Suzy Croft 'Citizen Involvement - a practical guide for Change' MacMillan 1993

(29) See chapters seven and eight in David Brandon 'Innovation without Change? consumer power in psychiatric services' MacMillan 1991

(30) Quoted in Peter Barham and Robert Hayward 'From the Mental Patient to the Person' Routledge 1991 (Pges 149-50)

(31) Ibid. (Pge 135)

(32) Christine Perring 'The Experience of Hospital Closure' Avebury 1993

(33) F. Reissman 'Restructuring Help: a human services for paradigm for the 1990s' American Journal of Community Psychology, 18, 1990 (Pges 221 - 230) quoted in Charles Rapp et al . 'Research Strategies for Consumer Empowerment of People with Severe Mental Illness' Social Work 38(6) 1993

(34) MIND 'MIND Guide to Advocacy in Mental Health - empowerment in action' 1992 (Pge 7)

(35) Anuradha Sayal 'Black Women and Mental Health' The Psychologist January 1990 (Pges 24-27)

(36) 'Ashworth Hospital Enquiry' HMSO. 1992 (Pges 148 - 151)
(37) Vicky Rippere and Ruth Williams (Editor) 'Wounded Healers - mental health workers experiences of Depression' John Wiley 1985
(38) Steve Dowson 'Moving with the Dance' Values into Action, 1991

EIGHT: COLLECTIVE ADVOCACY:

'It's all right to offend people.'

Salman Rushdie 'Face to Face',
BBC 2, 10 October 1994

LOBBYING

The practice of various sorts of individual advocacy often has wider implications which lead naturally on to collective - also sometimes called system or group-advocacy. Legal cases centred on the grievances of particular individuals can also have both the intention and effect of bringing about major changes in the law, affecting tens of thousands of people in similar situations. As we saw earlier, MIND's strategy in the 1970s was to pursue individual cases through the courts, right up to the European Court of Human Rights, not just to seek redress for one particular Broadmoor Hospital patient, but to have a general impact on the relevant statutes and a knock-on effect on conditions and staff behaviour within the services.

Likewise, individuals with a disability may not only learn to express their own wishes but become increasingly concerned with how the services they are using perform overall. They can see that many others are also suffering and improvements may come more quickly through combining with them to press in political ways. One early example dates from 1620. There is a record of a pamphlet, now sadly mislaid, entitled 'The Petition of the Poor Distracted People in the House of Bedlam' complaining of the conditions in that infamous asylum, featured in Shakespeare. (1) We don't know how effective their petition was, although it may still be too early to judge!

As we saw in an earlier chapter, there is a considerable confusion between self and collective advocacy processes. Both People First and Survivors Speak Out usually describe themselves as self-advocacy movements. It is clear that much of what they both do falls rather more under the umbrella of collective advocacy. A good deal of their activity focuses on pressing for better services; using the media; helping to train professionals. . . Wolfensberger distinguishes this process as 'not concerned with individual grievances, but with patterns of problems, difficulties, shortcomings, and possibly with class needs'. He argues, hardly surprisingly, that these collective advocacy bodies should be independent of any direct service provision. (2)

Vested interests on this level can be just as injurious as on the individual level.

Des Wilson, the best-known British social activist, links the art of campaigning with the process of collective advocacy. 'In my time I've been an advocate for the homeless and their rights to be treated compassionately; an advocate for our rights to breathe clean air, drink clean water and generally be protected from pollution; an advocate for our rights to information . . . and for much more . . . That's what pressure groups and lobbyists are. They're advocates.'(3) He has worked with many such groups in trying to change government policy on social and ecological issues. Here the term advocate is being used in a much wider sense than usual - to be a component of community action; a skill within lobbying. (4) This is not advocacy on behalf of an individual and often not even on behalf of a recognisable group like people with muscular dystrophy but to argue a principle, of clean air for example - in which the client is perhaps the planet.

If devalued individuals are to get a hearing, it is essential that they form groups. Remaining isolated they can rarely be heard. Their power source must increasingly lie in their numbers and activities. 'People cannot question the assumptions of the dominant groups in their society all by themselves. To formulate new ways of doing things and set them in motion they need the support of other people who share their perception of the world and help them to challenge the conventional wisdom: "a resistance movement" of some sort. Women have been quite successful in doing this. Black minorities in a white world have found it harder, but not impossible. Many other oppressed groups have yet to gain an effective hearing.' (5) If you cannot get admission to the club which everyone else attends, you must form one of your own. These clubs or groups have their own dangers; they can easily become a source of secondary stigma. There is a delicate balance between the risk of further stigmatisation and the positive gains coming from joint support and action.

Collective advocacy involves quite different skills and different settings from the work with individuals. The relevant tasks and processes are also usually very different. As Wilson reminds us, it comes closer to what is more usually described as 'community action'. It involves less emphasis on individual representation and much more on lobbying - pressing politicians and professionals for better and improved conditions, linked with increased resources. It focuses on general issues rather than on the problems of individuals.

It means a lot of committee work; taking the chair at meetings;

managing finances; writing up minutes; planning press handouts and media impact to influence policies and strategies; learning how to communicate ideas; negotiating and compromising; working in groups creatively; mounting successful campaigns. It is essentially structural and political; doing deals amid the balancing of competing interests.

Sometimes there is an almost seamless move from family advocacy to the more collective kind. A few years ago, I talked with some Woodlands Group mothers - all of whom had had children with disabilities incarcerated in the Woodlands institution, near Vancouver in Canada. Some parents had tried to pretend that their children were better off inside, but really they were neglected in a huge and grim institution. The staff seemed excessively secretive, defensive and obstructive. Collectively, through regular meetings, these parents realised that their sense of outrage was a legitimate reaction to the individual powerlessness that each experienced in struggling for the needs of their sons or daughters. They had lost control over their lives. The institution had total control over their disabled children. They began to meet and focus together on changing the service. They had to develop some formal organisation and also to specialise in different roles and responsibilities.

Initially some parents developed programmes of reform with help from liberated and sympathetic professionals. They aimed to improve Woodlands through advocacy systems, regular case reviews and quality evaluation and the like. The institution tried to co-opt them as it had done all other pressure groups; to make them part of its empire. It would suck them into the institutional committees and reviews and they would simply disappear.

In a dramatic meeting with the relevant government minister, they were offered large sums of money to reform the institution, rather like Christ's temptation on the mountain. Some powerful and more innovative parents realised they must turn their backs on the traditional service. Instead, they lobbied the minister for the cash for the individual families to spend on their disabled children rather than for the block, professionally controlled services. With the money in their hands, they could make the basic decisions about their children's lives. They began a long and largely successful campaign to get smaller and more community based services as well as for individualised funding which they called service brokerage. The infamous Woodlands institution finally closed a few years later, to the delight of most parents. (6)

DIVISIONS AND UNITY

There is a great diversity among the various user and carer movements. There are reformers, radicals and diverse positions in between just as in the 'Woodlands Group'. At best, they can form an uneasy alliance. They believe differing things about the roots of disability; about the potential of existing services; about what works in changing things for the better. (7) Some want to run their own services and practise empowerment. Others are more reformist and simply ask for greater involvement in service management. Yet others campaign for the alleviation of major social conditions like poverty and housing which have a direct and major impact on disability. They ask why it means in our society that to be disabled involves being poor. Others simply demand drastically improved health and social services and don't care who manages them or how. However, most groups can see that in the large campaigns like the one working towards the Disability Act, there are benefits for everyone in burying their differences, at least temporarily.

Relationships between the different groups have sometimes been not just difficult but actively hostile. The Disability Movement has had very mixed feelings about potential recruits coming from the mental health and learning difficulties sectors. It has its own internal problems of disablism which sometimes focuses on divisions between visible and invisible disability - sometimes called 'wheelchairism'. Also some people formally diagnosed as 'mentally ill' have seen their so-called problems entirely to do with others or to do with society in general. Some members of the deaf community, for example, have even rejected the whole label of disability.

Relationships with carers as we saw in the Family Advocacy chapter are often fraught. The priorities of families can be very different. Some mental health carers actively campaigned against the rundown of the psychiatric hospitals. Other Carer's Groups like Mencap or the National Schizophrenia Fellowship simply seek increased safety and security for their adult children, who play very little part in their deliberations. Whilst working with MIND in the 1980s, I recall the hostility we directed at (and got back with compound interest) Mencap, mainly a relatives organisation.

Scott comments about these divisions: 'In Britain, more than in the U.S.A. the disability lobby is divided. Differences in origin, funding, representation, size and approach need to be put aside. The criteria for joining the struggle for anti-discrimination legislation should be a real and resourced commitment and nothing else. Personal and organisational egos have no place.' (8) That kind of passionate exhortation may be commendable and even necessary but is not particularly effective. But there are some positive signs. The Disability Manifesto was signed by 13 major disability organisations. It pressed for anti-discrimination legislation; fresh disability benefits; new quality services in community care; better and more relevant health services; more appropriate and integrated education; more facilities for employment and training; improved housing; relevant public transport and leisure; and increased access to community resources to end the 'apartheid system'. (9)

The Americans got their Disability legislation, in part, through what Scott calls a 'rainbow alliance' which had roots in the Civil Rights movements for black Americans; the returning disabled veterans from the Vietnam War; the active involvement of the deaf community; partnerships with carers; working together with the business community . . . (10) 'Coalitions were made with the AIDS lobby, "grey power" groups representing elderly people and anybody who was in favour of comprehensive anti-discrimination legislation.' (11) This was a large and powerful lobby, run on a shoe string, capable of buttonholing most influential politicians and community leaders whoever or wherever they were.

A similar powerful focus for working together in the UK is the important struggle, so far unsuccessful, for a Civil Rights Act for disabled people. Take this example: 'Civil Rights campaigners are urging the Government to take another look at the estimated costs of implementing the Civil Rights (Disabled Persons) Bill in the wake of a new critique which claims huge errors were made in their calculation. The critique, launched at the House of Commons, says that the cost of implementation could be reduced from the estimated £17 billion to just £5 billion . . .'   It was claimed that the Government duplicated figures; failed to calculate economic advantages; included guestimates; assumed a short time span; omitted to acknowledge access work already completed; neglected to recognise potential savings; provided ill-informed estimates of the amount which could be spent on enforcing the Bill through the Commission.(12) This is a quote from RADAR's campaign for fresh legislation and the increasingly sophisticated lobbying by Disability Groups in Parliament. MPs received thousands of letters when the Bill was tossed out; media coverage was extensive and mostly positive. It was helped or hindered bizarrely by the fact that the leading disability campaigner - Victoria Scott - was the daughter of the recalcitrant government minister Nicholas Scott. Their family arguments made excellent headlines!

Disabled people's groups are working together both formally and informally on several fronts. Even old style charities like Barnardos and Mencap, with a much higher profile and infinitely better funded, co-operate with those mainly newer, smaller and aggressive organisations, increasingly 'owned' by disabled people. For example, there is regular information and campaigning over social security because such large numbers of disabled people live on Giro. To give one example: on the 'Incapacity for Work Bill' 1994, RADAR calculates who would be the losers in the proposed changes - 'Up to 280,000 people currently on Invalidity Benefit will lose entitlement within two years of the introduction of Incapacity Benefit.' (13)

As in this RADAR example, many important issues in the daily lives of disabled people have little to do with the responsibilities of health and social services departments. 'Community Care services are not the only priorities for disabled people . . . *other* concerns - appropriate housing, accessible transport, access to public buildings and personal safety - ranked higher than existing community care services. Without these other facilities, independent living "in the community" was simply not possible.'(14) Without these ingredients, genuine integration, using the same kinds of facilities that the rest of us ordinarily use, is simply a fantasy.

Sacks describes a seminal event in the history of the deaf community. 'The University of Gallaudet in Washington, DC, USA, the only deaf university in the world, appointed a new hearing president in 1988. In all it's 124 years it had never had a deaf president. The students barricaded the campus and closed down the university.' The faculty and staff supported the students and demanded the appointment of a deaf president and the resignation of the Board chairman who was reported to have said 'The deaf are not yet ready to function in the hearing world.'

The 1970s had seen the rise of 'Deaf Pride' but this occasion at Gallaudet was an opportunity for 'Deaf Power'. Deaf college students came from all over the country to support their fellow students and academics. More than 2,500 people marched slowly on the Capitol. Within a few days, the incoming and hearing President had resigned. A researcher noted: 'It's really remarkable, because in all my experience I've seen deaf people be passive and accept the kind of treatment that hearing people give them. I've seen them willing, or seem to be willing, to be "clients," when in fact they should be controlling things . . . now all at once there's been a transformation in the consciousness of what it means to be a deaf person in the world, to take responsibility for things.' The appointment of the new president was announced two days after and he was a deaf man. (15)

Another significant but very different example of collective advocacy comes also from the USA - the campaign against the attempt by the Reagan administration to de regulate the Education for All Handicapped Children Act 1975, which opened the doors of the nation's schools to children with disabilities. The campaign argued that this de-regulation threatened the education of millions of children. It mobilised tens of thousands of people to protest, to write letters to senators and congressman. This was a campaign in which parents were the major force.

After a tremendous assault, the government proposals were withdrawn in September 1982. 'Education Secretary Bell acknowledged the outpouring of protest by parents and especially mothers who acted by writing letters, gathering signatures on petitions, and testifying at the scheduled public hearings.' He noted somewhat wryly that the 'written comments and the information presented to the public hearing . . . represented nearly unanimous disapproval of several positions proposed by the Department'.(16)

There are several processes here which parallel the campaign for a Civil Rights Act in the UK. Different disability organisations are combining together, presenting a united front around a single issue. Through newsletters and meetings they raise the consciousness of their many members. They lobby politicians and civil servants; make telephone calls, attend hearings of various kinds, write tens of thousands of letters, make innumerable phone calls; use the media - radio, newspapers and TV - and organise petitions.

Disability groups also use legal process as a weapon to clarify their rights. One major and continuing battle for people with a physical disability is access. 'An important victory in the struggle for independent living was won early this year when a Supreme Court judge ruled that the Highland Terrace Garden apartments in Clifton, New Jersey, had to make three units barrier-free before being granted a certificate of occupancy. . . This ruling brought jubilation to the members of Disabled, Information, Awareness and Living (DIAL) - an organization of disabled citizens who had challenged the developer's claim that garden apartments were excluded from the barrier-free design code.' (17) Victory in this single case has wide implications for similar access issues throughout this state and the whole USA.

We worked with two groups of long stay residents - one in a local authority hostel and another in a psychiatric hospital - both in the north-west of England. We tried to develop some increased consciousness of their situation. They lived in appalling conditions: poor food and oppressed by nursing staff. In summing up ward life, one resident said: 'No wine, no women and the radiogram is broken.' There was hardly any real consultation with residents in either place; an overall atmosphere of suffocating paternalism; only the hospital had an advocacy service - a Citizens Advice Bureau - however none of the ward residents knew of its existence, even though it was located only twenty five yards away from the entrance to their ward. After publication of our booklet, there was a four year break in contact with the hospital in which we were vilified as troublemakers by some staff. Over the next few years, all our recommendations on consultation and advocacy were accepted. We are still banned, as far as we know, from the local authority hostel. (18)

Increasingly, devalued groups use the media for campaigning. For example, Survivors Speak Out campaigned against the public advertising of the newly formed mental illness charity SANE, calling it both insulting and degrading. In June 1989, it organised an important meeting of about thirty service users with the then Shadow Health Minister, Robin Cook, MP to influence Opposition policy on mental health issues. (19) It is now regularly consulted by the Department of Health. Last year, it was consulted about supervised discharge; at risk registers and the use of seclusion in special hospitals. The recently established Royal College of Psychiatrists Patients' Liaison Group provides a setting for MINDLINK, UKAN (United Kingdom Advocacy Network) and the Manic Depression Fellowship to meet with representatives from the psychiatric profession. (20)

With this breakthrough come the attendant dangers of co-option. Groups seeking radical changes in the balance of power can get sucked into the existing power imbalance and be simply used and manipulated. They seek acceptance and influence. They must get close enough to be heard and to influence; too close and they get co-opted into the existing systems. Illich writes about the impact of co-option on the Catholic Church when it became a state agency in the giving out of funds to the poor. 'By becoming an "official" agency of one kind of progress, the Church ceases to speak for the underdog who is outside the agencies but who is an ever growing majority . . . Money thus builds the Church a "pastoral" structure beyond its means and makes it a political power.'(21)

These diverse groups also need support themselves. The National Advocacy Network was set up in 1990 to back up groups like Survivors Speak Out, working for greater user involvement in the mental health services. 'Part of the work of the Network will consist of providing an up to date picture of how user involvement is developing across the country, where and how it is successful and where it needs greater attention and resources.' It received some funding to set up a national office in Nottingham. (22)

There is also the growth of more specialised groups to press forward on behalf of other neglected groups. 'Womankind' was set up in Bristol in 1985 to promote mental health in women. 'It is a multiracial project which aims to confront racism, oppressive stereotypes and prejudices of all kinds. The first open meeting of Women and Mental Health brought together well over 50 women and the impetus grew from there. Monthly meetings were held in different parts of Bristol; a day workshop attended by more than a 100 women provided a forum where women's experiences of mental health services were shared.' (23)

Developing groups also challenge inherent racism. 'Nafsiyat challenges many of the preconceptions which have been traditionally associated with "psychotherapy" and "trans-cultural psychiatry": that ethnic and cultural minorities are unsuitable for therapy, that payment is always necessary for successful therapy; that it requires long term commitment with frequent attendance. It also requires workers to re-examine their own definition of cultural and racial issues as well as their own personal way of working.' (24) There are a number of problems in involving people from ethnic minorities in user collectives. 'There are obstacles to the full involvement of black and minority ethnic groups and people with disabilities.' (25)

The future seems to lie, at least partly, in separate and distinct Black and ethnic forums such as those in the London borough of Haringey. (26)

Patient councils, an important idea imported from the Netherlands, are a vital expression of collective advocacy. Dutch councils gained specific legal roles. For example, they have powers of veto over items like ward re decorations or any kind of research involving patients. (27) Nottingham Patients Council Support Group (NPCSG) pioneered councils in January 1986 and employed a Dutch development worker. (28) At present the group supports councils in Mapperley Hospital, Queens Medical Centre, day centres, hospitals and community mental health centres. (29)

NPCSG set out four basic aims: to create more awareness and control by users of services; to create user-only meetings in services and to support the issues they raised; to influence planning and management of mental health services; to educate workers both locally and nationally about the need for use involvement. Every month, representatives of the hospital management attend the Council meeting to discuss outstanding issues and to act on them. (30)

ISSUES

Berry argues about increasing the 'effectiveness of lobbying'. He outlines three elements:- 'the goal of citizen groups should be to become *institutionalized* into the administrative policy-making process' but not *'at the price of being co-opted by government officials'* and *'resources ought to be generally allocated toward informal lobbying* and away from formal citizen participation programs.' (31) He argues that most such programmes are ineffective but that does not deter the various campaigners. 'Making hearings "interactive" or ensuring that advisory boards are more "representative," is not likely to make much difference to ultimate policy outcomes.'(32) What is the real impact of collective advocacy on services and more especially the lives of disabled individuals?

Some observers are extremely ambivalent. 'The process is circular: without power, you will not be heard; but until you are heard, you cannot influence the basis of consent to the power you seek. community action . . has largely failed, in the short run, because it had no power to alter the priorities of attention. But from its frustrations arose a movement to protest the right of the poor and all politically disadvantaged minorities to be heard, which over a decade has profoundly influenced our conceptions of democracy.'(33)

The Care in the Community legislation encouraged increased consultation with and involvement in policy making by users and carers, not only on an individual level but also on a more systemic one. Now that is being fundamentally questioned. 'A growing uncertainty over the purpose of community care planning is likely to threaten both the commitment of disabled people to take part in consultation and undermine the impact of the contribution they make . . . If purchasing services, setting service specifications and monitoring quality are all entirely separate from the process of community care planning, then it is difficult see any purpose for the latter, other than perhaps giving information on services and how to obtain them.' (34)

Collective advocacy tries to maintain an extremely difficult balance. How do these organisation stay close to the mandate given them by disabled people and avoid becoming part of the lobby circus? How do you impact on powerful and often hostile organisations which impose their own concept of 'reality'' and also control most of the money? How do you influence them without making them even more hostile and defensive? The media is a crucial ingredient in this process but newspapers, radio and TV are increasingly controlled and influenced by these same defensive organisations which gradually increase their news manipulation skills.

References:

(1) Dale Peterson (Editor) 'A Mad People's History of Madness' University of Pittsburgh Press, (Page 47) and see also Shakespeare's 'King Lear' - for example Tom O' Bedlam.

(2) Wolf Wolfensberger 'A Multi-component advocacy/protection schema' Canadian Association for the Retarded' 1977 (Pge 59-60)

(3) Des Wilson 'Campaigning - the A-Z of public advocacy' Hawkesmere 1993

(4) See for example Alan Twelvetrees 'Community Work' MacMillan 1982

(5) David Donnison 'A Radical Agenda'Rivers Oram Press, 1991 (Pge 193)

(6) Taken from David Brandon 'Direct Power' Tao 1991 (Pge 2)

(7) Helen Smith 'Collaboration for Change' in David Towell *et al.* 'Managing Psychiatric Services in Transition' King's Fund College 1989

(8) Victoria Scott 'Lessons from America - a study of the Americans with a Disability Act' RADAR 1994 (Pge 39)

(9) 'Disability Manifesto - an agenda for the 1990s' RADAR and twelve other disability organisations, 1991

(10) Richard K. Scotch in 'Politics and Policy in the History of the Disability Rights Movement' The Millbank Quarterly: vol 67, Supplement 2, Part 2 1989 (Pges 380-400) suggests that this involved less than a total of 100,000 people with disabilities.

(11) Victoria Scott Ibid. (Pges 18-19)

(12) RADAR Bulletin: 'Take another look at costs - campaigners tell Government' no 239 July 1994

(13) RADAR Bulletin: 'Social Security' no 239 July 1994

(14) Catherine Bewley and Caroline Glendinning 'Involving disabled people in community care' Joseph Rowntree Foundation, 1994 (Pge 36)

(15) Oliver Sacks 'Seeing Voices' Picador 1989 (chapter three)

(16) James McCullagh 'Challenging the proposed deregulation of P.L. 94-142: a case study of collective advocacy' Journal of Sociology and Social Welfare, 15 (Pges 65-81)

(17) Eileen van Kirk 'Two Victories in one Ruling' Accent on Living, Winter 1985

(18) Althea and David Brandon 'Consumers as Colleagues' MIND 1987

(19) David Brandon 'Innovation without Change?' (Chapter Seven) MacMillan 1991

(20) Peter Campbell 'Royal College of Psychiatrists' liaison group' Survivors Speak Out newsheet June 1994 (Pge 3)

(21) Ivan Illich 'Celebration of Awareness' Penguin Education, 1973 (Pge 52)

(22) National Advocacy Network: post 1991 conference pack: January 1992,

(23) Woman in MIND 'Finding our own solutions - women's experiences of mental health care' MIND 1986

(24) Sourangshu Acharyya *et al.* 'Nafsiyat: a psychotherapy centre for ethnic minorities' Psychiatric Bulletin 13, 1989 (pages 358-60)

(25) Tessa Jowell 'Community Care - a prospectus for the task' Rowntree Foundation, 1991

(26) Nirveen Kalsi and Pamela Constantinides 'Working towards racial equality in health care - the Haringey experience' King's Fund Centre 1989

(27) Hans Wiegant 'Users' Councils in Holland' Asylum 2 April 1988

(28) Nottingham Patient's Councils Support Group 'Information Pack' 1990

(29) Colin Gell in Liz Winn (Editor) 'Power to the People' Kings Fund 1990

(30) 'The MIND Guide to Advocacy in Mental Health - empowerment in Action' MIND 1992 (Pge 15)

(31) Jeffrey Berry 'Beyond Citizen Participation: effective advocacy before administrative agencies' The Journal of Applied Behavioural Science, vol (17, no 4, 1981 (Pges 463-477)

(32) Ibid. (Pge 466)

(33) Peter Marris and Martin Rein 'Dilemmas of Social Reform' Pelican, 1974 (Pges 363-4)

(34) Catherine Bewley and Caroline Glendinning 'Involving disabled people in community care' Joseph Rowntree Foundation, 1994 (Pge 36)

NINE: CONCLUSION

*'We learn, when we respect the dignity of the people, that
they cannot be denied the elementary right to participate
fully in the solutions to their own problems. Self respect
arises only out of people who play an active role in solving
their own crises and who are not helpless, passive, puppet-
like recipients of private or public services. To give people
help, while denying them a significant part in the action,
contributes nothing to the development of the individual. In
the deepest sense, it is not giving but taking - taking their
dignity. Denial of the opportunity for participation is the
denial of human dignity and democracy. It will not work.'*
(1)

We have covered four major elements in this short textbook on
advocacy with people who have disabilities:

* **raising consciousness**
* **developing advocacy skills and appropriate structures**
* **opening doors so that services are more participative**
* **establishing clear rights and redress.**

We are gradually laying the foundations of **consciousness raising**
which involves considerable obstacles. Freire wrote powerfully of
the 'fear of freedom . . . a fear which may equally well lead them to
desire the role of oppressor or bind them to the role of oppressed,
should be examined'. (2) He was arguing for a much greater awareness of oppression; of the infinite possibilities of freedom and the
fear that accompanies it. Hundreds of thousands of individuals are
largely unaware of being oppressed - they are socially and economi-
cally marginalised, live in huge institutions, eat poor food, live in
poverty, are often physically and sexually abused. They need to be
awakened.

I recall having a pizza with a man who had spent eight years in a
horrible mental handicap hospital. He talked of the time when the
charge nurse had thrown his glasses to the ground and stamped on
them. His eyes filled with tears and even weeks later he was still so
rageful about this and a hundred other incidents. He was frightened
of the powerful feelings inside. Even though he had been 'out in the
community' for several years, he still carried that deep fear and
related it to the group home staff where he now lived. (3)

His life was still meaningless; a round of routine and mostly boring activities. He lived in the community, isolated from his neighbours, really knowing few people; with no job; training irrelevant to anything outside the world of disability. Warner comments accurately about mental illness: 'The institutional neurosis has been replaced by an existential neurosis which is the product of the psychotic person's alienation in the community. Meaninglessness is one of the core existential concerns which confronts any individual, and many people with mental illness face lives of profound purposelessness. Their days are empty of productive activity, their social relationships are few and often dependent and unrewarding. According to Salvador Maddi, among others, existential neurosis, in its most severe form, presents as chronic aimlessness, meaningless and apathy coupled with boredom, depression and loss of a sense of personal value and mastery.' (4) My friend was an expert in this; what the psychoanalysts call the 'everyday trauma of eventlessness'.

The major role in creating this fresh consciousness must lie with those who have direct experiences, through the process of self-advocacy. Their professional allies must comprehend this. 'Disability training needs to challenge common myths, to demonstrate the practical application of equal opportunities . . . to recognise the discriminatory language and the visual images that help to perpetuate the inequality of disabled people.'(5)

There are huge tasks in the areas where people are doubly and trebly discriminated against. Commenting on the implementation of Care in the Community, Mussenden writes: '. . . there are two areas where you cannot claim "so far so good", namely with regard to Black communities and carers. . . The traditional difficulties faced by all carers have persisted, such as the lack of appropriate respite care/day care/family care, sitter services and the lack of emergency cover in the event of ill health. Many of the improvements for Black carers within the community care reforms have not materialised. There is still a lack of: specific projects targeting Black carers; basic information; comprehensive advice systems, specific points of contact or carers' liaison worker; counselling services or preventive work to relieve the stress of caring.' (6) We have seen some evidence of the difficult struggle to include a variety of devalued groups like ethnic minorities, gays and lesbians.

We must develop both **appropriate skills and structures** for advocacy. In citizen advocacy, the Management Boards present serious problems because they tend to be white and able-bodied.

They are 'owned' by the dominant and most oppressive group. It is crucial that disabled people take over the whole process themselves as an effective check on the imperialistic ambitions of the various professionals.

There is a considerable neglect and even a complete absence of relevant training in the necessary skills, paradoxically in the very areas of nursing and social work where some professional observers claim the central ground. If they are going to advocate or at the least have a relevant role, then good training is essential. It needs to confront inherent disablism in able-bodied people. There is a healthy spread of good quality training of professionals by some disabled groups. If professionals are going to be effective allies then they need to be much more skilful and knowledgeable.

Advocacy remains essentially fragile and vulnerable and needs considerable protection. It is carried on the backs of a comparatively few individuals who are continually under attack. They make criticism of structures and systems and mostly get back personal abuse. Wolfensberger reminds us: 'Why is advocacy vulnerable? The answer lies partly in the "cosmic reality" of entropy. Good things are apt to get worse, not better. A second part of the answer is the enmity of the moral nature of advocacy. All sorts of dynamics push moral endeavour away, and devalues certain people. Hence, most welfare service bureaucracies discriminate, and victimise people, with government sanction via funding and legal structures, despite the presence of good people who work within them. These services control the lives of vulnerable people.'(7)

He suggests eight clusters of safeguards:

'*   understanding what advocacy is and how it differs from
      other good things
 *   understand how important advocacy is, and being committed
      to it
 *   to know the reality and meaning of standing in contradiction
 *   to take attacks for granted, and safeguard against them
 *   to understand internal and external stresses on advocacy
      efforts, especially seduction, mutually antagonistic
      functions and fear
 *   to be suspicious of "imperial" schemes to benefit needy
      people
 *   to recognise support and protect legitimate advocacy forms
 *   to accept the finiteness and imperfections of any and all
      human enterprises.' (9)

It is useless if we develop effective advocacy systems and the services remain or become even more defensive than at present. The **doors must be opened** even wider so that many more people may share in the overall policy making. The personal costs of the various whistleblowers are an eloquent testimony to the excessive defensiveness of the different institutions. We have a few wounds and scars ourselves. We need to develop systems which are much more responsive to service users and their allies and hopefully involve less-emotional costs.

That is a huge challenge. 'Practitioners must be willing to identify consumers as the primary informants about what is wanted and needed from providers. They must be willing to elevate consumers from the role of client(s) to the roles of teacher and partner in a collective learning enterprise.'(9) The movement towards greater participation involves a fresh partnership between the relatively powerful and the powerless. That is always a difficult process. Power is rarely given or shared freely; it must usually be taken.

There are some good signs. There is a growing interest in involving service users and carers in both planning and management. For example, the North West Thames Regional Health Authority commissioned People First to evaluate aspects of its hospital closure programme; to look at the movement of people out of hospital into the community. It was a unique piece of work - the very first time that people with learning difficulties have evaluated a service in this country. (10)

However, before we get too ecstatic, only 12% of social services departments reported carrying out any consultation at all - through meetings, workshops or surveys - before writing the draft of their 'care in the community' plan. Often disabled organisations were given very little time for consultation. Few plans indicated where changes had been made after consultation. Information in braille, on tape, in large print or in languages other than English was usually only produced at this later stage when the major decisions had been made. (11)

There is a big push towards **rights for people with disabilities**. The Americans have established a comprehensive Disability Act and European people with disabilities, especially the British, want to follow suit. So far, this pressure has not succeeded other than becoming a major unifying force for the embryonic Disability Movement. Whatever the problems in applying the empowerment principles, the youthful advocacy movement has recorded some early successes.

'The patients' rights movement shows that the direct action of a relatively powerless group can have significant effects on overall social policy, even if its success in part depends upon the support of more powerful groups intent on co-option. . .   While sympathetic professionals might prefer a more polite form of strategy, it is probably necessary to have the sharp level of criticism and action provided by the patients' movement as a complement to mainstream reform. . .   The fact that patients' rights issues are often pressed by a powerless group takes the direction of reform somewhat out of the hands of policy makers and higher level professionals.' (12) It is this powerful combination of disabled outsiders and inside professionals which is so very effective.

One element in any fresh openness must lie in the more effective handling of complaints; offering people easier and more effective means to redress wrongs. Most local and health authorities seemingly have excellent procedures. However, in reality, complainants are frequently made to feel guilty, even as if they are on trial. Sometimes it feels like storming the Bastille. They are combating deeply ingrained patterns of territoriality; they are outsiders awakening the aggressive desires of those besieged inside to repel all boarders. Tunnard suggests some alternative strategies:

* an acknowledgement that something has occurred which is regretted;
* an explanation of the investigation;
* an apology for any shortcomings identified;
* an explanation of how these have been or will be remedied, and when and how changes can be checked;
* an expression of thanks for having given feedback; and
* how the matter can be pursued further if the user wishes to do so. (14)

Rights give an important expression to values embodying concepts of equality of opportunity. One contemporary problem is the domination of both planning and management by so-called pragmatic considerations.   "One of the commonplace "facts" about current restructuring of welfare policy is that it has been undertaken almost entirely on the basis of economic pragmatism. Such pragmatic views reject both the former rhetoric of grand political visions and its implicit value structure which supported the theory of citizenship. Perhaps one of the dominant aspects of the welfare state "crisis" debate, and of the successes of the neo-conservative rejection of the role of values, is that it has not really been a debate." (14)

On a more fundamental level, the block exists in the pathologisation of individuals rather than in a perception of whole systems. In that context the participation of the patient/client, any feedback at all - particularly critical - becomes an unnecessary nuisance. 'Professionals in health planning and health services have become accustomed to thinking about people mostly as sources of pathology, or victims of pathology, and consequently as a "target" for preventive and therapeutic services. In effect, we have come to accept a negative view of people's role in health; we blame them for getting themselves into trouble, for delaying in seeking care, for "foolish" beliefs and practices, and for not "complying" with medical regimes. This perspective is part of a professional-industrial construction of reality that differentiates between providers of health services, who have the necessary medical knowledge and skills, and consumers of health services, who have problems and precious little else.' (15)

It would be tragic if the whole advocacy movement became just another aspect of the professionalisation of ordinary human life, including disability; that it became another service with all its many products taken out of the control of people with disabilities. Seabrook comments wryly and wisely as usual: 'The presence of armies of advisers, counsellors and therapists at the scene of every human and social catastrophe is just another example of the professionalising of grief, the expropriation and processing of human emotions, after the model of any other industry, like canning fish or adding value to semi-finished goods from the factory. It brings forth a new division of labour, which gives an impression of a society advancing, caring; whereas the truth is that much of this consists of what is largely privatised economic activity masquerading as something else; and that something else is part of the priceless capacity of human beings to create and offer things to each other freely.' (16)

A shift towards advocacy brings no panacea but a fresh set of problems. This book hopefully suggests that these problems might be not only different but involve some kind of improvement for service users. As always these issues are fundamentally spiritual. Will the egotism of the advocates be any less than that of the social workers, psychiatrists, therapists, etc. Probably not. Will we gain wisdom inside ourselves and also inside the systems? Skynner reminds us that 'many of us "sneak" into caring or therapeutic agencies by the staff door to get psychological help without acknowledging the need for it'.(17)

Many professionals, and I include myself, are vicarious clients. We must continue to look very closely at our motives in helping others. (18) 'In general, the power drive is given freest rein when it can appear under the cloak of objective and moral rectitude. People are the most cruel when they can use cruelty to enforce the "good".'(20) We must maintain contact with our deep shadow side otherwise we will become so destructive in work with others. The movement towards advocacy can take us away from the essential personal pilgrimage which is at the root of real love and genuine wisdom and lead us to project all that is horrible and destructive onto others and the agencies which employ them.

The immense danger is that we change from being indirect clients to being rescuers with or without a white horse. In advocacy, the rescuer mode presents a deep temptation; rescuers need desperately to find victims. That has great costs for the victims. The distressed damsel in medieval history was probably better off taking her chances with the dragon. After being rescued by the knight she spent most of her life bored rigid in castles and neglected because her spouse went off for years to The Crusades. In our advocacy, we must struggle hard to promote the autonomy of the customers rather than our own self-centred wishes and the colonialist ambitions of our professions; to avoid reductionist concepts like 'victims'. That is very easy to write but has proved extremely hard to practise.

References

(1) Saul Alinsky 'Rules for Radicals - a pragmatic primer for realistic radicals' Vintage (N.Y.) 1972
(2) Paulo Freire 'Pedagogy of the Oppressed' Penguin Education 1972 (Pge 23)
(3) David Brandon 'Strange Places' University College Salford, 1991
(4) Richard Warner in Shula Ramon (Editor) 'Beyond Community Care - normalisation and integration work' MacMillan 1991
(5) K. Gillespie-Sells and J. Campbell 'Disability Equality Training: trainers guide' London Boroughs Disability Resource Team and CCETSW June 1991 (Pge 7)
(6) Barry Mussenden 'Community Care and Black Carers' Talkback, January 1994
(7) Wolf Wolfensberger 'Citizen Advocacy Principles and Perversions' World Citizen Advocacy Congress: Lincoln, Nebraska, 6 Oct 1991 (Pge 1)
(8) Ibid. (Pge 7)
(9) Charles A. Rapp *et al.* 'Research Strategies for Consumer Empowerment of People with Severe Mental Illness' Social Work 38(6) 1993, Pge 733

(10) Andrea Whittaker, Simon Gardner and Joyce Kershaw 'Service evaluation by people with learning difficulties' Kings Fund 1991

(11) Catherine Bewley and Caroline Glendinning 'Involving disabled people in community care planning' Rowntree Foundation, 1994 (Pge 12)

(12) Phil Brown (editor) 'Mental Health Care and Social Policy' Routledge 1985, (Pge 207)

(13) Jo Tunnard 'Righting Wrongs' Community Care, 25 November 1993

(14) Ian Culpitt 'Welfare and Citizenship - beyond the crisis of the Welfare State?' SAGE 1992 (Pges 183-4)

(15) Lowell S. Levin 'Self Care in Health: Potential and Pitfalls' World Health Forum - an international journal of Health Development, WHO. Vol. 2, No 2, 1981

(16) Jeremy Seabrook 'Vested Disinterests' New Statesman and Society, 20 May 1994 (Pge 14)

(17) Robin Skynner 'Institutes and how to survive them - mental health training and consultation' Tavistock 1989 (Pge 158)

(18) see my own 'Zen in the Art of Helping' Penguin Arkana 1990

(19) Adolf Guggenbühl-Craig 'Power in the Helping Professions' Spring Publications, USA, 1971 (Pge 10)